W9-BJV-624

Presented to

_____

By

_____

On the Occasion of

_____

Date

_____

Guide
to the
Bible

A Genesis to Revelation
tour of God's Word

G. E. Dean

BARBOUR
PUBLISHING, INC.
Uhrichsville, Ohio

Guide
to the
Bible

ISBN 1-57748-666-8

All Scripture quotations are taken from the King James Version of the Bible.

Published by Barbour Publishing, Inc., P.O. Box 719, Uhrichsville, OH 44683 http://www.barbourbooks.com

Member of the
Evangelical Christian
Publishers Association

Printed in the United States of America.

INTRODUCTION

The Bible is the Book written by God that tells us about God. Throughout the thirty-nine books of the Old Testament and twenty-seven books of the New Testament, God tells us of His love, wisdom, power, and forgiveness. God also describes our desperate need for Him.

My desire is that this devotional guide will lead you to the Book and to the God of the Book. We must move away from self-centeredness to God-centeredness. God is our ultimate need, and the Bible, an oasis in a dry and barren land. It is food for the soul. God's Word is timeless because it is truth. All Bible verses included in this devotional guide have been taken from the King James Version of the Bible. The Books are listed just as they appear in the Bible in order to encourage you to get into your Bible and read it. In addition, a topical index of pertinent subjects follows for easy reference. By delving into a certain topic, you can quickly see the relevancy of Scripture for everyday life.

May God richly use this little book to help many.

G. E. DEAN

Genesis

*In the beginning God created the heaven
and the earth.*
GENESIS 1:1

God has always been. There has never been a
time when He was not. Put your life into the
capable hands of the God of the Bible.

—⁂—

*So God created man in his own image,
in the image of God created he him;
male and female created he them.*
GENESIS 1:27

You're no accident. You have been created in the
image of God. God has a wonderful plan for you.

And the LORD God formed man
of the dust of the ground,
and breathed into his nostrils
the breath of life;
and man became a living soul.
GENESIS 2:7

Humanity is God's crowning creation. He breathed a living soul into us so that we may have fellowship with Him.

—◦◦◦—

Now the serpent was more
subtle than any beast of
the field which the LORD God had made.
And he said unto the woman,
Yea, hath God said,
Ye shall not eat of every tree of the garden?
GENESIS 3:1

The devil loves to cast doubt on God's Word. Do not listen to the devil. Trust God and His Word.

And the LORD said unto Cain,
Where is Abel thy brother? And he said,
I know not: Am I my brother's keeper?
GENESIS 4:9

We are to be concerned about one another. When we see a person in need, we should not look the other way. We are our brothers' keepers!

———

And Enoch walked with God:
and he was not; for God took him.
GENESIS 5:24

Enoch walked with God, but God was the One who was leading. Let the Lord guide your life.

———

And the LORD said,
My spirit shall not always strive with man,
for that he also is flesh:
yet his days shall be an hundred and twenty years.
GENESIS 6:3

Don't take God for granted. Say yes to Him now while you have the opportunity.

> *And Noah did*
> *according unto all that*
> *the LORD commanded him.*
> GENESIS 7:5

What would happen if more men and women lived like Noah? The world needs to see people who really love the Lord.

> *And they said,*
> *Go to,*
> *let us build us a city and a tower,*
> *whose top may reach unto heaven;*
> *and let us make us a name,*
> *lest we be scattered abroad upon*
> *the face of the whole earth.*
> GENESIS 11:4

We are not here to make a name for ourselves. People will probably never speak our names one hundred years from now. We are here to honor God and be a blessing to others. That's what will last forever.

Abram dwelled in the land of Canaan,
and Lot dwelled in the cities of the plain,
and pitched his tent toward Sodom.
But the men of Sodom were wicked
and sinners before the LORD exceedingly.
GENESIS 13:12–13

Be careful where you plant your life. It makes a difference.

―∾∾―

And he believed in the LORD;
and he counted it to him for righteousness.
GENESIS 15:6

Faith in God is what really pleases Him. Faith in God is what really blesses us. Have faith in God!

―∾∾―

And when Abram was ninety years old and nine,
the LORD appeared to Abram,
and said unto him, I am the Almighty God;
walk before me, and be thou perfect.
GENESIS 17:1

We never get too old to hear and obey the Lord. We need Him every day of our lives.

> *And Lot went out,*
> *and spake unto his sons in law,*
> *which married his daughters,*
> *and said, Up, get you out of this place;*
> *for the LORD will destroy this city.*
> *But he seemed as one that mocked*
> *unto his sons in law.*
> GENESIS 19:14

Lot's sons-in-law lost their lives because they did not take God seriously. Don't make the same mistake.

—————

> *And while he lingered,*
> *the men laid hold upon his hand,*
> *and upon the hand of his wife,*
> *and upon the hand of his two daughters;*
> *the LORD being merciful unto him:*
> *and they brought him forth,*
> *and set him without the city.*
> GENESIS 19:16

Just as the Lord was merciful to Lot and his family, He will be merciful to you, too. Grab ahold of the Lord and let Him lead your life.

And Abraham called the name
of that place Jehovah-jireh:
as it is said to this day,
In the mount of the LORD it shall be seen.
GENESIS 22:14

Abraham made the wonderful discovery that God is a good provider. You can discover this, too. Trust the Lord with all your heart.

———

And Isaac digged again the wells of water,
which they had digged in the days
of Abraham his father;
for the Philistines had stopped them
after the death of Abraham:
and he called their names after
the names by which his father
had called them.
GENESIS 26:18

As Isaac went back to his father's wells, so we need to go back to our ancestors' deep roots of faith.

And he lifted up his eyes,
and saw the women and the children;
and said, Who are those with thee?
And he said, The children which God
hath graciously given thy servant.
GENESIS 33:5

Children are a gift and blessing from God. What are we doing with these precious lives? Be the parents God wants you to be.

———

Then Jacob said unto his household,
and to all that were with him,
Put away the strange gods that are among you,
and be clean, and change your garments:
And let us arise, and go up to Beth-el;
and I will make there an altar unto God,
who answered me in the day of my distress,
and was with me in the way which I went.
GENESIS 35:2–3

Let's pray for something similar to take place today: "Lord, send a revival."

And when his brethren saw
that their father loved him
more than all his brethren,
they hated him,
and could not speak peaceably unto him.
GENESIS 37:4

Hatred and bitterness will destroy you. Don't let these take root in your life. Fill your life with love for God and others.

———

And Pharaoh said unto his servants,
Can we find such a one as this is,
a man in whom the Spirit of God is?
And Pharaoh said unto Joseph,
Forasmuch as God hath showed thee all this,
there is none so discreet
and wise as thou art.
GENESIS 41:38–39

Oh, how we need to be a people that are filled and led by the Spirit of God! We have the answers that the world desperately needs to hear.

And God sent me before you to
preserve you a posterity in the earth,
and to save your lives by a great deliverance.
GENESIS 45:7

God has a plan for His people and, if you pay attention, you will see it. God is always at work.

———

The sceptre shall not depart from Judah, nor a
lawgiver from between his feet, until Shiloh come;
and unto him shall the gathering of the people be.
GENESIS 49:10

This is a definite reference to the Messiah since Jesus was from the tribe of Judah. God always keeps His Word.

———

But as for you, ye thought evil against me;
but God meant it unto good,
to bring to pass, as it is this day,
to save much people alive.
GENESIS 50:20

God specializes in turning lemons into lemonade. The trouble you're having today may turn out to be a blessing tomorrow.

Exodus

And God looked upon the children of Israel,
and God had respect unto them.
EXODUS 2:25

God is still looking out for His people. Cast your
cares upon Him. He loves you.

———ᨀ———

And when the LORD saw that
he turned aside to see,
God called unto him out of the midst of the bush,
and said, Moses, Moses.
And he said, Here am I.
EXODUS 3:4

Are you ready to listen to God? Are you ready to
obey?

And God said unto Moses,
I AM THAT I AM:
and he said,
Thus shalt thou say unto the children of Israel,
I AM hath sent me unto you.
EXODUS 3:14

God never changes. He is the great, eternal, time-less One. You can depend on Him.

———

And Moses said unto the LORD, O my Lord,
I am not eloquent, neither heretofore,
nor since thou hast spoken unto thy servant:
but I am slow of speech,
and of a slow tongue.
And the LORD said unto him,
Who hath made man's mouth?
or who maketh the dumb, or deaf,
or the seeing, or the blind?
have not I the LORD?
EXODUS 4:10–11

If we are not careful, excuses to God will cause us to miss many blessings. God would not command us to do something that could not be done. Have faith and obey the Lord.

And Pharaoh said, Who is the LORD,
that I should obey his voice to let Israel go?
I know not the LORD,
neither will I let Israel go.
EXODUS 5:2

Pharaoh didn't know who God was at first. But he knew Him very well by the time of the exodus. God is on the throne.

—⁕—

Wherefore say unto
the children of Israel,
I am the LORD,
and I will bring you out from under
the burdens of the Egyptians,
and I will rid you out of their bondage,
and I will redeem you
with a stretched out arm,
and with great judgments.
EXODUS 6:6

God kept His promise to Israel and He will keep His promises to you. God never changes. "Jesus Christ the same yesterday, and to day, and for ever" (Hebrews 13:8).

But when Pharaoh saw
that there was respite,
he hardened his heart,
and hearkened not unto them;
as the LORD had said.
EXODUS 8:15

Don't harden your heart toward the Lord. If you do, you will be the loser.

———

And the blood shall be to you for
a token upon the houses where ye are:
and when I see the blood,
I will pass over you,
and the plague shall not be upon you
to destroy you,
when I smite the land of Egypt.
EXODUS 12:13

The New Testament counterpart of the blood on the doorpost is the shed blood of Jesus Christ on the cross. "What can wash away my sin? Nothing but the blood of Jesus."

And the LORD went before them
by day in a pillar of a cloud,
to lead them the way;
and by night in a pillar of fire,
to give them light;
to go by day and night.
EXODUS 13:21

The Lord is still the expert in leading lives. He will guide you if you let Him. Why not give Him control now of your life?

———

The LORD shall fight for you,
and ye shall hold your peace.
EXODUS 14:14

Let the Lord fight your battles. Just follow and obey Him. He will take care of the enemy.

———

The LORD shall reign for ever and ever.
EXODUS 15:18

Kings and rulers come and go, but the Lord reigns forever and ever. This gives life its proper perspective.

And [Moses] said, If thou wilt diligently hearken
to the voice of the LORD thy God,
and wilt do that which is right in his sight,
and wilt give ear to his commandments,
and keep all his statutes,
I will put none of these diseases upon thee,
which I have brought upon the Egyptians:
for I am the LORD that healeth thee.
EXODUS 15:26

He is still the same wonderful Lord. Let Him bring healing to your mind, soul, and body. He is Lord. Seek Him and experience His blessings.

—∾∾∾—

But Moses' hands were heavy;
and they took a stone, and put it under him,
and he sat thereon;
and Aaron and Hur stayed up his hands,
the one on the one side,
and the other on the other side;
and his hands were steady until
the going down of the sun.
EXODUS 17:12

Your pastor and other spiritual leaders need your help and encouragement. Be there for them. God will use you.

Thou shalt have no other gods before me.
EXODUS 20:3

There is only one true God. Worship Him and Him alone.

—⁓—

Honour thy father and thy mother:
that thy days may be long upon the land
which the LORD thy God giveth thee.
EXODUS 20:12

We need a refresher course on this commandment. Parents, let's teach our children to respect authority.

—⁓—

Thou shalt not bear false witness
against thy neighbour.
EXODUS 20:16

Gossip and backbiting are strictly forbidden by the Word of God. As one man said, "He that slings mud loses a lot of ground." Treat your neighbor with respect.

Thou shalt not covet thy neighbour's house,
thou shalt not covet thy neighbour's wife,
nor his manservant, nor his maidservant,
nor his ox, nor his ass,
nor any thing that is thy neighbour's.
EXODUS 20:17

Coveting is the sin that sets many other sins in motion. Philippians 4:8 is a good remedy: "Finally, brethren, whatsoever things are true, whatsoever things are honest, whatsoever things are just, whatsoever things are pure, whatsoever things are lovely, whatsoever things are of good report; if there be any virtue, and if there be any praise, think on these things."

―❦―

Thou shalt not raise a false report:
put not thine hand with the wicked
to be an unrighteous witness.
EXODUS 23:1

Gossip and lying hurt all involved. Speak the truth and be a blessing.

Thou shalt not follow a
multitude to do evil;
neither shalt thou speak
in a cause to decline after
many to wrest judgment.
EXODUS 23:2

Don't follow the crowd. Stand up for the Lord. You will be a blessing when you do.

―∽∾―

And he [Moses] took
the book of the covenant,
and read in the audience of the people:
and they said,
All that the LORD hath said
will we do,
and be obedient.
EXODUS 24:7

If this happened today in the congregations of God's people, there would certainly be revival. The key word is "all." We can't pick and choose what we like. We must simply obey the Lord because He knows what is best.

Then Moses stood in the gate of the camp,
and said, Who is on the LORD'S side?
let him come unto me.
And all the sons of Levi gathered
themselves together unto him.
EXODUS 32:26

Quit walking on the fence. Stand up for the Lord and be counted.

And all the people saw
the cloudy pillar stand
at the tabernacle door:
and all the people
rose up and worshipped,
every man in his tent door.
And he [Moses] said unto him,
If thy presence go not with me,
carry us not up hence.
EXODUS 33:10, 15

Moses knew the importance of God's presence in his life. We should not go where God would not go.

Take heed to thyself,
lest thou make a covenant with
the inhabitants of the land whither thou goest,
lest it be for a snare in the midst of thee.
EXODUS 34:12

Be careful to surround yourself with godly people.
Alliances with the ungodly will cause trouble.

—∞—

And they came,
every one whose heart stirred him up,
and every one whom his spirit made willing,
and they brought the LORD'S offering to
the work of the tabernacle of the congregation,
and for all his service,
and for the holy garments.
EXODUS 35:21

Is God stirring your heart now? Give your life to
Him. You'll be glad you did.

Leviticus

And it shall be,
when he shall be guilty in one of these things,
that he shall confess that
he hath sinned in that thing.
LEVITICUS 5:5

To confess means to agree with God that you have done wrong. When you do this, God can work. Unload your guilt on the One who can set you free.

———

The fire shall ever be burning upon the altar;
it shall never go out.
LEVITICUS 6:13

Is the fire of the Lord burning in your heart? Don't let it die. Stoke God's fire with prayer and Bible study.

*For I am the LORD that bringeth you up
out of the land of Egypt, to be your God:
ye shall therefore be holy, for I am holy.*
LEVITICUS 11:45

God's people are to be holy. The glory of God should be seen in the way we live our lives.

———∽∾∽———

*Ye shall not steal, neither deal falsely,
neither lie one to another.*
LEVITICUS 19:11

If we would only return to God and His ways our world would be so much better. "Lord, send a revival of honesty and integrity to our land."

———∽∾∽———

*Thou shalt not avenge,
nor bear any grudge against
the children of thy people,
but thou shalt love thy neighbour as thyself:
I am the LORD.*
LEVITICUS 19:18

Grudges destroy. Love and forgiveness breathe life. Will you hold onto the past or reach out for an everlasting future?

Thou shalt rise up
before the hoary head,
and honour the face
of the old man,
and fear thy God:
I am the LORD.
LEVITICUS 19:32

We need a revival of respect for the elderly. Let's honor those who are older than we are.

And when ye reap
the harvest of your land,
thou shalt not make clean riddance of
the corners of thy field when thou reapest,
neither shalt thou gather any
gleaning of thy harvest:
thou shalt leave them unto the poor,
and to the stranger:
I am the LORD *your God.*
LEVITICUS 23:22

Leave some of your income to help those in need. Selfishness is the plague of our day. Look around you. You'll be blessed for your generosity.

And all the tithe of the land,
whether of the seed of the land,
or of the fruit of the tree,
is the LORD'S: it is holy unto the LORD.
LEVITICUS 27:30

One-tenth of our earnings should go to the Lord. He owns it all anyway. "The earth is the LORD'S, and the fulness thereof; the world, and they that dwell therein" (Psalm 24:1).

Numbers

The LORD bless thee,
and keep thee:
The LORD make his face shine upon thee,
and be gracious unto thee.
NUMBERS 6:24–25

Have a good day with God's help.

And Moses said unto them,
Stand still, and I will hear what
the LORD will command concerning you.
NUMBERS 9:8

What good advice. We must have times of quiet so that we may seek the Lord and His will. Are you taking time to be still and know God's will?

At the commandment of the LORD
they rested in the tents,
and at the commandment of the LORD
they journeyed:
they kept the charge of the LORD,
at the commandment of the LORD
by the hand of Moses.
NUMBERS 9:23

God gives us directions for our lives because He loves us. Life would make so much more sense if you simply obeyed the Lord. See how your life comes together when you do what God wants you to do.

—⁓—

And it shall be, if thou go with us,
yea, it shall be,
that what goodness
the LORD shall do unto us,
the same will we do unto thee.
NUMBERS 10:32

Blessings from God are meant to be shared. Have you been blessed in a special way? Share it with someone else.

(Now the man Moses was very meek,
above all the men which were
upon the face of the earth.)
NUMBERS 12:3

God uses humble people. Can God use you?

———

But they presumed to go up
unto the hill top:
nevertheless the ark of
the covenant of the LORD,
and Moses,
departed not out of the camp.
Then the Amalekites came down,
and the Canaanites
which dwelt in that hill,
and smote them,
and discomfited them,
even unto Hormah.
NUMBERS 14:44–45

Presumption can lead to disaster. Have faith in God and you will see the victory.

Out of all your gifts ye shall offer
every heave offering of the LORD,
of all the best thereof,
even the hallowed part
thereof out of it.
NUMBERS 18:29

The Lord deserves your very best. Are you giving Him that?

———

And Moses made a serpent of brass,
and put it upon a pole,
and it came to pass,
that if a serpent had bitten any man,
when he beheld the serpent of brass,
he lived.
NUMBERS 21:9

This is an obvious reference to John 3:14: "And as Moses lifted up the serpent in the wilderness, even so must the Son of man be lifted up." Jesus died on the cross for our sins. Place your faith in Him and experience sins forgiven and the promise of eternal life.

God is not a man, that he should lie;
neither the son of man,
that he should repent: hath he said,
and shall he not do it?
or hath he spoken,
and shall he not make it good?
NUMBERS 23:19

God said it and that settles it, whether we believe it or not. God can't lie. You can depend on Him and on His Word, the Bible.

———✦———

And the LORD spake unto Moses, saying,
Phinehas, the son of Eleazar,
the son of Aaron the priest,
hath turned my wrath away
from the children of Israel,
while he was zealous for my sake among them,
that I consumed not the children of
Israel in my jealousy.
Wherefore say,
Behold, I give unto him my covenant of peace.
NUMBERS 25:10–12

Don't be half-hearted for the Lord. Give Him your heart and experience His peace.

Surely none of the men
that came up out of Egypt,
from twenty years old and upward,
shall see the land which
I sware unto Abraham,
unto Isaac, and unto Jacob;
because they have not wholly followed me:
Save Caleb the son of Jephunneh the Kenezite,
and Joshua the son of Nun:
for they have wholly followed the LORD.
NUMBERS 32:11–12

Are you following the Lord with your whole heart? When you do, blessings will come. Follow the Lord completely.

———

But if ye will not do so,
behold, ye have sinned against the LORD:
and be sure your sin will find you out.
NUMBERS 32:23

Sin has its payday. Repent and ask God's forgiveness, which is the only hope for humankind.

But if ye will not drive out
the inhabitants of the land from before you;
then it shall come to pass,
that those which ye let remain
of them shall be pricks in your eyes,
and thorns in your sides,
and shall vex you in the land wherein ye dwell.
NUMBERS 33:55

Do you struggle with such personal "inhabitants" as selfishness, greed, jealousy, and bitterness? Don't tolerate these. Ask the Lord to rid you of these enemies.

Deuteronomy

Then I said unto you, Dread not,
neither be afraid of them.
The LORD your God which goeth before you,
he shall fight for you,
according to all that he did for you
in Egypt before your eyes.
DEUTERONOMY 1:29–30

The Lord will help you. Surrender your life and circumstances to Him.

———

Ye shall not fear them:
for the LORD your God he shall fight for you.
DEUTERONOMY 3:22

God takes care of His own. Don't be afraid. Leave your problems in His hands.

Only take heed to thyself,
and keep thy soul diligently,
lest thou forget the things which
thine eyes have seen,
and lest they depart from thy heart
all the days of thy life:
but teach them thy sons,
and thy sons' sons.
DEUTERONOMY 4:9

Parents, don't forget God's many blessings. Be sure to pass them on to your children. They will be sources of blessing in years to come.

Know therefore this day,
and consider it in thine heart,
that the LORD
he is God in heaven above,
and upon the earth beneath:
there is none else.
DEUTERONOMY 4:39

This is the Lord's universe. He will not share His glory with another. "This is the day which the LORD hath made; we will rejoice and be glad in it" (Psalm 118:24).

O that there were such an heart in them,
that they would fear me,
and keep all my commandments always,
that it might be well with them,
and with their children for ever!
DEUTERONOMY 5:29

Do you have a heart that pleases God? When an obedient heart pleases God, blessings for you and your family abound.

Ye shall observe to do therefore as
the LORD your God
hath commanded you:
ye shall not turn aside to
the right hand
or to the left.
DEUTERONOMY 5:32

Obeying God should not be done in a sloppy, half-hearted manner. It makes a difference to Him. Obedience to God shows that we love Him. "If ye love me, keep my commandments" (John 14:15). Give your best for the Lord.

Hear, O Israel:
The LORD our God is one LORD:
And thou shalt love the LORD thy God
with all thine heart,
and with all thy soul,
and with all thy might.
DEUTERONOMY 6:4–5

The Lord deserves and expects our best. He is worthy to be loved, worshiped, and served.

And thou shalt teach them diligently
unto thy children,
and shalt talk of them when
thou sittest in thine house,
and when thou walkest by the way,
and when thou liest down,
and when thou risest up.
DEUTERONOMY 6:7

Are you teaching your children the ways of the Lord? It is imperative that they learn about the Lord when they are young. Don't wait any longer. Let them see the Lord in your life and actions.

And he humbled thee,
and suffered thee to hunger,
and fed thee with manna,
which thou knewest not,
neither did thy fathers know;
that he might make thee know that
man doth not live by bread only,
but by every word that proceedeth out of
the mouth of the LORD doth man live.
DEUTERONOMY 8:3

Difficult times can be a blessing. They remind us that God, and He alone, can be trusted no matter what happens. Read the Bible and stand on God's promises. "Thy word have I hid in mine heart, that I might not sin against thee" (Psalm 119:11).

Thou shalt also consider in thine heart,
that, as a man chasteneth his son,
so the LORD thy God chasteneth thee.
DEUTERONOMY 8:5

The Lord disciplines those He loves. That's how we know we really belong to Him.

And now, Israel,
what doth the LORD
thy God require of thee,
but to fear the LORD thy God,
to walk in all his ways,
and to love him,
and to serve the LORD thy God
with all thy heart
and with all thy soul.
DEUTERONOMY 10:12

If you're wondering what God wants from you, read this verse. Respect the Lord by obeying His word and by serving Him with loving devotion. This is the life that pleases God.

———

Every man shall give as he is able,
according to the blessing of the LORD
thy God which he hath given thee.
DEUTERONOMY 16:17

Do you only receive from God? The Bible says that we should gladly give back to God, too.

And the LORD thy God will make thee
plenteous in every work of thine hand,
in the fruit of thy body,
and in the fruit of thy cattle,
and in the fruit of thy land,
for good: for the LORD will again
rejoice over thee for good,
as he rejoiced over thy fathers.
DEUTERONOMY 30:9

God wants to bless His people. Our responsibility is to trust and obey Him. Remember, our Heavenly Father knows what is best for us.

———

Be strong and of a good courage,
fear not, nor be afraid of them:
for the LORD thy God,
he it is that doth go with thee;
he will not fail thee,
nor forsake thee.
DEUTERONOMY 31:6

Faith in God will sustain you through the hard times. Nothing else can compare.

And the LORD,
he it is that doth go before thee;
he will be with thee, he will not fail thee,
neither forsake thee:
fear not, neither be dismayed.
DEUTERONOMY 31:8

Don't be afraid. The Lord is going ahead of you. He will never leave or forsake those who love Him.

———∞———

And he said unto them,
Set your hearts unto all the words
which I testify among you this day,
which ye shall command your children
to observe to do, all the words of this law.
For it is not a vain thing for you;
because it is your life:
and through this thing ye shall
prolong your days in the land,
whither ye go over Jordan to possess it.
DEUTERONOMY 32:46–47

The Word of God is not just a collection of sayings. The Word of God is life itself. Take time to read the Bible today. Happiness comes when we believe and obey.

Thy shoes shall be iron and brass;
and as thy days,
so shall thy strength be.
DEUTERONOMY 33:25

God will give you the strength you need. Give Him today and every day.

Joshua

Now after the death of Moses
the servant of the LORD it came to pass,
that the LORD spake unto Joshua
the son of Nun, Moses' minister, saying,
Moses my servant is dead;
now therefore arise, go over this Jordan,
thou, and all this people,
unto the land which I do give to them,
even to the children of Israel.
There shall not any man be able to stand
before thee all the days of thy life:
as I was with Moses,
so I will be with thee:
I will not fail thee, nor forsake thee.
JOSHUA 1:1–2, 5

God is faithful. He will always be there for His
own. Do you know the Lord?

This book of the law shall not
depart out of thy mouth;
but thou shalt meditate therein
day and night,
that thou mayest observe to do
according to all that is written therein:
for then thou shalt make
thy way prosperous,
and then thou shalt have good success.
JOSHUA 1:8

Here's the key to real peace and success. Every serious disciple of the Lord should have a Bible reading plan. Do you have one? Meditate on God's Word and then obey it.

Have not I commanded thee?
Be strong and of a good courage;
be not afraid, neither be thou dismayed:
for the LORD thy God is with thee
whithersoever thou goest.
JOSHUA 1:9

Don't be afraid. The Lord will take care of you. Put your situation into God's capable hands.

And Joshua said unto the people,
Sanctify yourselves:
for tomorrow the LORD will
do wonders among you.
JOSHUA 3:5

Are you preparing yourself for God to do great things in and through you? Have a sensitive heart for the things of God.

———

That this may be a sign among you,
that when your children ask
their fathers in time to come,
saying, What mean ye by these stones?
Then ye shall answer them,
That the waters of Jordan were cut off before
the ark of the covenant of the LORD;
when it passed over Jordan,
the waters of Jordan were cut off:
and these stones shall be for a memorial
unto the children of Israel for ever.
JOSHUA 4:6–7

Are our children seeing evidence of the Lord's work in our lives? Share with your children what the Lord means to you.

So the people shouted when
the priests blew with the trumpets:
and it came to pass,
when the people heard the sound of the trumpet,
and the people shouted with a great shout,
that the wall fell down flat,
so that the people went up into the city,
every man straight before him,
and they took the city.
JOSHUA 6:20

God can use anybody to accomplish His purposes. Remember: The people shouted and the walls of Jericho came tumbling down.

———

And the men took of their victuals,
and asked not counsel
at the mouth of the LORD.
JOSHUA 9:14

We are headed for trouble when we forget to seek the mind of the Lord. Before you decide an issue, ask yourself this question: "Have I prayed about it?"

> *As the LORD commanded Moses his servant,*
> *so did Moses command Joshua,*
> *and so did Joshua;*
> *he left nothing undone of all that*
> *the LORD commanded Moses.*
> JOSHUA 11:15

Are we leaving any of God's business undone? If so, let's repent and follow the example of Moses and Joshua. Obey the Lord.

> *Hebron therefore became*
> *the inheritance of Caleb*
> *the son of Jephunneh*
> *the Kenezite unto this day,*
> *because that he wholly followed*
> *the LORD God of Israel.*
> JOSHUA 14:14

God blesses those who wholly follow Him. "But my God shall supply all your need according to his riches in glory by Christ Jesus" (Philippians 4:19).

Did not Achan the son of Zerah
commit a trespass in the accursed thing,
and wrath fell on all the congregation of Israel?
and that man perished not alone in his iniquity.
JOSHUA 22:20

Sin never occurs in a vacuum. It always affects others. Is your life a blessing or a curse to those around you? Be a blessing, not a stumbling block.

———

And, behold,
this day I am going
the way of all the earth:
and ye know in all your hearts
and in all your souls,
that not one thing hath failed
of all the good things which
the LORD your God
spake concerning you;
all are come to pass unto you,
and not one thing hath failed thereof.
JOSHUA 23:14

God is faithful. He always keeps His promises.

And if it seem evil unto you to serve the LORD,
choose you this day whom ye will serve;
whether the gods which your fathers served
that were on the other side of the flood,
or the gods of the Amorites,
in whose land ye dwell:
but as for me and my house,
we will serve the LORD.
JOSHUA 24:15

Have you made your choice? Choose the Lord today and every day and life will be worth the living.

Judges

And ye shall make no league with
the inhabitants of this land;
ye shall throw down their altars:
but ye have not obeyed my voice:
why have ye done this?
JUDGES 2:2

God's people cannot compromise with sin and be
a blessing. Is your life counting for the Lord?

And the people served the LORD
all the days of Joshua,
and all the days of the elders that outlived Joshua.
JUDGES 2:7

Godly leadership is a blessing to families, towns,
and nations. May God give us men and women
who love the Lord to lead us in the days to come.

And also all that generation were
gathered unto their fathers:
and there arose another generation after them,
which knew not the LORD,
nor yet the works which
he had done for Israel.
JUDGES 2:10

While your parents may have been or are believers, each new generation must personally come to know the Lord. Thus the question becomes: Do you know Him?

———

And he said unto him,
Oh my Lord,
wherewith shall I save Israel?
behold, my family is poor in Manasseh,
and I am the least in my father's house.
JUDGES 6:15

Even though Gideon thought he was a nobody, look at what God did through him! Don't limit God. Let Him work in your life, too.

And the LORD said unto Gideon,
The people that are with thee are too many
for me to give the Midianites into their hands,
lest Israel vaunt themselves against me, saying,
Mine own hand hath saved me.
JUDGES 7:2

God doesn't need great numbers to get the job done. With just a handful of people He can accomplish much. The key is dedication. Can God count on you?

———

And Gideon said unto them,
I will not rule over you,
neither shall my son rule over you:
the LORD shall rule over you.
JUDGES 8:23

Godly leadership is marked by humility and loving service. We must point people to the Lord and not ourselves. Serve the Lord and others with all your heart and give God the glory.

And they put away the strange gods
from among them,
and served the LORD:
and his soul was grieved
for the misery of Israel.
JUDGES 10:16

God sympathizes with the pain you are experiencing. When you hurt, He hurts. Seek the Lord and see what He can do to help you. No one cares for you like the Lord.

—∞—

And she [Delilah] said,
The Philistines be upon thee, Samson.
And he awoke out of his sleep,
and said, I will go out as at other times before,
and shake myself.
And he wist not that the LORD
was departed from him.
JUDGES 16:20

It is so easy to drift away from the Lord. Often we don't even realize it until we have gone far away. Is this you? If so, return to the One who loves you.

Ruth

And Ruth said, Intreat me not to leave thee,
or to return from following after thee:
for whither thou goest, I will go;
and where thou lodgest, I will lodge:
thy people shall be my people,
and thy God my God.
RUTH 1:16

We need more love and loyalty in our lives today, and a good place to begin is at home. Take time to love your family.

And Jesse begat David.
RUTH 4:22

This genealogy is important because it shows God's faithfulness in eventually providing the Messiah, Jesus, from the seed of David. You can count on God to keep His word.

1 Samuel

The Lord killeth, and maketh alive:
he bringeth down to the grave, and bringeth up.
The Lord maketh poor, and maketh rich:
he bringeth low, and lifteth up.
1 Samuel 2:6–7

Obviously the Lord is not someone to be ignored. Put your life and your future in His hands.

For I have told him that I will judge his house
for ever for the iniquity which he knoweth;
because his sons made themselves vile,
and he restrained them not.
1 Samuel 3:13

Parents, are we doing all we can do to encourage our children to live for the Lord? We have an awesome responsibility.

And Samuel spake unto all the house of Israel,
saying, If ye do return unto the LORD
with all your hearts,
then put away the strange gods
and Ashtaroth from among you,
and prepare your hearts unto the LORD,
and serve him only:
and he will deliver you out of
the hand of the Philistines.
Then the children of Israel did
put away Baalim and Ashtaroth,
and served the LORD only.
1 SAMUEL 7:3–4

We need this kind of revival in our land. "Lord, send a revival."

—∞—

Moreover as for me,
God forbid that I should sin against
the LORD in ceasing to pray for you:
but I will teach you the good
and the right way.
1 SAMUEL 12:23

Are you praying for those who are a part of your life? You would want them to be praying for you.

Only fear the LORD,
and serve him in truth with all your heart:
for consider how great things he hath done for you.
1 SAMUEL 12:24

Why shouldn't we want to serve the Lord? He has been so good to us. "Serve the Lord with gladness."

———

But now thy kingdom shall not continue:
the LORD hath sought him a man
after his own heart,
and the LORD hath commanded him
to be captain over his people,
because thou hast not kept that
which the LORD commanded thee.
1 SAMUEL 13:14

The Lord is still looking for those who have a heart for Him. Can He count on you?

———

For there is no restraint to the LORD
to save by many or by few.
1 SAMUEL 14:6

The Lord can do great things with a few as well as with many. Be one of the faithful and watch God use you.

And Samuel said,
Hath the LORD as great delight
in burnt offerings and sacrifices,
as in obeying the voice of the LORD?
Behold, to obey is better than sacrifice,
and to hearken than the fat of rams.
1 SAMUEL 15:22

The Lord is more concerned about our hearts and obedience than He is about religious ritual. Worship and serve the Lord "in spirit and in truth."

———✦———

But the LORD said unto Samuel,
Look not on his countenance,
or on the height of his stature;
because I have refused him:
for the LORD seeth not as man seeth;
for man looketh on the outward appearance,
but the LORD looketh on the heart.
1 SAMUEL 16:7

The Lord focuses more on the inside than on our outward appearances. Is your heart in tune with the Lord?

> *The LORD that delivered me*
> *out of the paw of the lion. . .*
> *he will deliver me.*
> 1 SAMUEL 17:37

It pays to remember the victories of the past that God has given you. It will give you faith and courage to face the future.

———∿∿———

> *And all this assembly shall know that*
> *the LORD saveth not with sword and spear:*
> *for the battle is the LORD'S,*
> *and he will give you into our hands.*
> 1 SAMUEL 17:47

The Lord will give you the victory also. Turn that struggle over to the Lord now.

———∿∿———

> *And Jonathan Saul's son arose,*
> *and went to David into the wood,*
> *and strengthened his hand in God.*
> 1 SAMUEL 23:16

A child of God may need some encouragement from you today. It may be your pastor, Sunday school teacher, or next-door neighbor. Encourage them as Jonathan encouraged David.

And David was greatly distressed;
for the people spake of stoning him,
because the soul of all the people was grieved,
every man for his sons and for his daughters:
but David encouraged himself
in the LORD his God.
1 SAMUEL 30:6

When life gets tough, follow David's example. Draw your strength from the Lord.

2 Samuel

And it came to pass after this,
that David inquired of the LORD, saying,
Shall I go up into any of the cities of Judah?
And the LORD said unto him, Go up.
And David said, Whither shall I go up?
And he said, Unto Hebron.
2 SAMUEL 2:1

Before you make that decision, ask the Lord. Everyone needs His wisdom and guidance. Take your decision to the Lord in prayer.

———ᴧᴧ———

O LORD God. . .there is none like thee.
2 SAMUEL 7:22

It is good to remind ourselves of the greatness and faithfulness of God. It is also good to share this with others.

And David said,
Is there yet any that is left of the house of Saul,
that I may show him kindness for Jonathan's sake?
2 SAMUEL 9:1

Are we looking to do acts of kindness for others or are we just waiting for others to do them for us?

———

For thou didst it secretly:
but I will do this thing before all Israel,
and before the sun.
2 SAMUEL 12:12

We cannot hide sin from God. He knows, and at times He reveals it to the world. It is imperative that God's people live holy lives.

———

I have sinned against the LORD. . .
The LORD also hath put away thy sin;
thou shalt not die.
2 SAMUEL 12:13

Confession of sin will open the way to God's forgiveness. "If we confess our sins, he is faithful and just to forgive us our sins, and to cleanse us from all unrighteousness" (1 John 1:9).

> *Howbeit, because by this deed*
> *thou hast given great occasion*
> *to the enemies of the LORD to blaspheme,*
> *the child also that is born unto thee*
> *shall surely die.*
>
> 2 SAMUEL 12:14

All sin has consequences. Large sins often have large consequences. May we never give God's enemies an occasion to blaspheme His name.

———❧———

> *But now he is dead, wherefore should I fast?*
> *can I bring him back again?*
> *I shall go to him,*
> *but he shall not return to me.*
>
> 2 SAMUEL 12:23

David spoke these words after the death of his baby boy. Here's a promise to all who have lost little children: They have gone on to heaven and if we know the Lord, we will join them.

And the afflicted people thou wilt save:
but thine eyes are upon the haughty,
that thou mayest bring them down.
2 SAMUEL 22:28

God has the final say on people. He honors the humble and brings down the haughty.

And the king said unto Araunah, Nay;
but I will surely buy it of thee at a price:
neither will I offer
burnt offerings unto the LORD my God
of that which doth cost me nothing.
So David bought the threshingfloor
and the oxen for fifty shekels of silver.
2 SAMUEL 24:24

Real love for God means sacrificial giving. When we practice this, our lives are enriched.

1 Kings

And keep the charge
of the LORD thy God,
to walk in his ways,
to keep his statutes,
and his commandments,
and his judgments,
and his testimonies,
as it is written in the law of Moses,
that thou mayest prosper
in all that thou doest,
and whithersoever thou turnest thyself.
1 KINGS 2:3

God gives His word to us for our own good. Fulfillment in life comes from obeying the teachings of the Lord. Apply Bible truths to your life and enjoy the abundant life of God.

*Give therefore thy servant an
understanding heart to judge thy people,
that I may discern between good and bad:
for who is able to judge
this thy so great a people?*
1 KINGS 3:9

The Lord will give wisdom to those who ask. The answer to your problems may be just a prayer away. Are you willing to obey what God speaks to your heart?

———

*And God gave Solomon wisdom
and understanding exceeding much,
and largeness of heart,
even as the sand
that is on the sea shore.*
1 KINGS 4:29

What our world needs is not more facts and figures but "largeness of heart." Don't be selfish. Open your heart to a world that needs love. God will give you the power to make a wonderful difference.

Then hear thou in heaven
thy dwellingplace,
and forgive, and do,
and give to every man
according to his ways,
whose heart thou knowest;
(for thou, even thou only,
knowest the hearts of
all the children of men;).
1 KINGS 8:39

You can't hide your heart from God. He knows all about you. Even with this knowledge, God still loves and cares about you. God is so good!

———

Blessed be the LORD,
that hath given rest unto his people Israel,
according to all that he promised:
there hath not failed one word of
all his good promise,
which he promised by the hand of
Moses his servant.
1 KINGS 8:56

You can put your trust in the Lord. He keeps His promises. As you do, don't forget to praise the Lord for His faithfulness.

And Solomon did evil
in the sight of the LORD,
and went not fully after the LORD,
as did David his father.
1 KINGS 11:6

I wonder how many Solomons there are today who have not followed in the footsteps of godly parents. Are you one? If so, turn your life around. One of the greatest blessings of life is to have godly parents whose example can be followed.

And Elijah came unto
all the people,
and said,
How long halt ye between two opinions?
if the LORD be God, follow him:
but if Baal, then follow him.
And the people answered him
not a word.
1 KINGS 18:21

You can't walk the fence with God. Either you serve Him or you serve another. Decide to follow the Lord. It's the best way to go.

> *Yet I have left me*
> *seven thousand in Israel,*
> *all the knees which*
> *have not bowed unto Baal,*
> *and every mouth which*
> *hath not kissed him.*
> 1 KINGS 19:18

You may think you're alone in serving the Lord, but you're not. You're part of the great army of God.

> *And Ahab said to Elijah,*
> *Hast thou found me, O mine enemy?*
> *And he answered, I have found thee:*
> *because thou hast sold thyself to*
> *work evil in the sight of the LORD.*
> 1 KINGS 21:20

Is your life full of God's goodness or full of evil? Don't sell out to sin and greed. Serve the Lord. Only He can bring real joy to your life.

*And Jehoshaphat said
unto the king of Israel,
Inquire, I pray thee,
at the word of the LORD to day.*
1 KINGS 22:5

Ask the Lord for wisdom before you make that decision. He knows what is best for you.

—⁓—

*And he did evil in the sight of the LORD,
and walked in the way of his father,
and in the way of his mother,
and in the way of Jeroboam
the son of Nebat,
who made Israel to sin.*
1 KINGS 22:52

Parents, we must realize that our children will follow our habits, both good and bad. What kind of example are you?

2 Kings

*And this is but a light thing
in the sight of the LORD:
he will deliver the Moabites also into your hand.*
2 KINGS 3:18

Our God is able to do great things for His people. Don't make the Lord too small in your eyes. Believe that He can do what He says.

———∿———

*And his servants came near, and spake unto him,
and said, My father, if the prophet had
bid thee do some great thing,
wouldest thou not have done it?
how much rather then, when he saith to thee,
Wash, and be clean?*
2 KINGS 5:13

It's the little things that most often hinder us. We must learn to obey God in all areas.

And he answered, Fear not:
for they that be with us are more than
they that be with them.
2 KINGS 6:16

God's people never stand alone. He is always with them. The Holy Spirit is in you and the host of heaven obey God's beck and call.

Then they said one to another,
We do not well:
this day is a day of good tidings,
and we hold our peace:
if we tarry till the morning light,
some mischief will come upon us:
now therefore come,
that we may go
and tell the king's household.
2 KINGS 7:9

Good news is meant to be shared. As the people of God, we have the best news in the world. Share with others what the Lord has done for you.

And he did that which was right
in the sight of the LORD:
he did according to all that his father
Uzziah had done.
2 KINGS 15:34

What a blessing it is to have a godly father!
Father, if your son followed your example, what
kind of man would he be?

———

And the children of Israel
did secretly those things that were not right
against the LORD their God,
and they built them high places
in all their cities,
from the tower of the watchmen
to the fenced city.
2 KINGS 17:9

You can't hide sin from God. He knows all. "And
as it is appointed unto men once to die, but after
this the judgment" (Hebrews 9:27). Repent and
let God forgive.

Notwithstanding
they would not hear,
but hardened their necks,
like to the neck of their fathers,
that did not believe
in the LORD their God.
2 KINGS 17:14

Do you have a rebellious spirit toward God? A hard heart is a terrible condition of the soul. God has a better way. Repent, and then love and serve the Lord. God loves you.

And Hezekiah received the letter
of the hand of the messengers,
and read it:
and Hezekiah went up into
the house of the LORD,
and spread it before the LORD.
2 KINGS 19:14

Do you have a problem? Go "up into the house of the Lord" and spread it before Him. He can do something about it.

In those days was
Hezekiah sick unto death.
And the prophet Isaiah the son of Amoz
came to him, and said unto him,
Thus saith the LORD,
Set thine house in order;
for thou shalt die, and not live.
2 KINGS 20:1

Death is certain. Is your house in order? Commit your life to the Lord and it will be.

———

And it came to pass,
when the king had heard the words
of the book of the law,
that he rent his clothes.
2 KINGS 22:11

Here is a key: We must take time to listen to the Word of God. King Josiah was convicted of his sin when he heard the Word of the Lord. We need that kind of repentance and humility today. "Lord, send a revival."

Because thine heart was tender,
*and thou hast humbled thyself before the L*ORD,
when thou heardest what I spake
against this place,
and against the inhabitants thereof,
that they should become a desolation and a curse,
and hast rent thy clothes, and wept before me;
*I also have heard thee, saith the L*ORD.
2 KINGS 22:19

The Lord hears those who have responsive hearts
toward Him. Are you listening to what God is
saying to you?

———

And like unto him was there no king before him,
*that turned to the L*ORD *with all his heart,*
and with all his soul, and with all his might,
according to all the law of Moses;
neither after him arose there any like him.
2 KINGS 23:25

"Lord, give us leaders like Josiah. Help us to
stand behind those who stand for You."

1 Chronicles

And Jabez called on the God of Israel,
saying, Oh that thou wouldest bless me indeed,
and enlarge my coast,
and that thine hand might be with me,
and that thou wouldest keep me from evil.
1 CHRONICLES 4:10

May God raise up men and women who will pray with a bold, holy faith. May God bless you, but more importantly, may He make you a blessing.

Then said Saul to his armourbearer,
Draw thy sword,
and thrust me through therewith. . . .
But his armourbearer would not.
1 CHRONICLES 10:4

Never do something you know to be wrong.

And of the children of Issachar,
which were men that had
understanding of the times,
to know what Israel ought to do;
the heads of them were two hundred;
and all their brethren were
at their commandment.
1 CHRONICLES 12:32

May God give us the wisdom to understand the times in which we live. We certainly need His help. "Trust in the LORD with all thine heart; and lean not unto thine own understanding. In all thy ways acknowledge him, and he shall direct thy paths" (Proverbs 3:5–6).

And the ark of God remained with the family of
Obed-edom in his house three months.
And the LORD blessed the house of Obed-edom,
and all that he had.
1 CHRONICLES 13:14

Blessings come to the homes of those who honor God's presence. Is the Lord a welcomed guest in your home?

And it shall be,
when thou shalt hear a sound of
going in the tops of the mulberry trees,
that then thou shalt go out to battle:
for God is gone forth before thee
to smite the host of the Philistines.
1 CHRONICLES 14:15

It is comforting to know that God goes before us to fight our battles. Listen to what God is saying and follow Him. That is the key to victory.

———

Then on that day David delivered
first this psalm to thank the LORD
into the hand of Asaph and his brethren.
1 CHRONICLES 16:7

All of God's people are what we are by the grace of God. If we must brag, let's brag on the Lord.

———

And to stand every morning to
thank and praise the LORD,
and likewise at even.
1 CHRONICLES 23:30

Try this twice-daily exercise that really refreshes. Stand and praise the Lord!

And thou, Solomon my son,
know thou the God of thy father,
and serve him with a perfect heart
and with a willing mind:
for the LORD searcheth all hearts,
and understandeth all the
imaginations of the thoughts:
if thou seek him,
he will be found of thee;
but if thou forsake him,
he will cast thee off for ever.
1 CHRONICLES 28:9

More godly men should be having heart-to-heart talks with their sons. As fathers, it's one of our greatest privileges.

2 Chronicles

Give me now wisdom and knowledge,
that I may go out and come in before this people:
for who can judge this thy people, that is so great?
2 CHRONICLES 1:10

Solomon prayed for wisdom more than anything else. Our Lord is willing to give us wisdom as well, if we just ask.

As the trumpeters and singers were as one,
to make one sound to be heard
in praising and thanking the LORD. . .
then the house was filled with a cloud,
even the house of the LORD.
2 CHRONICLES 5:13

The unity of God's people in praising Him is an awesome wonder. Praise the Lord!

If my people, which are called by my name,
shall humble themselves, and pray,
and seek my face,
and turn from their wicked ways;
then will I hear from heaven,
and will forgive their sin,
and will heal their land.
2 CHRONICLES 7:14

We need a revival in our world and this is the way we can get it. Let's pay the price for revival.

For he took away
the altars of the strange gods,
and the high places,
and brake down the images,
and cut down the groves:
And commanded Judah to seek
the LORD God of their fathers,
and to do the law and the commandment.
2 CHRONICLES 14:3–4

Are you allowing altars to strange gods to be built in your life? Take them away. Love and serve the Lord with all your heart.

And all Judah rejoiced at the oath:
for they had sworn with all their heart,
and sought him with their whole desire;
and he was found of them:
and the LORD gave them rest round about.
2 CHRONICLES 15:15

Peace comes to people when they seek the Lord with all their hearts. Are you troubled? Seek Him! He is the Prince of Peace.

For the eyes of the LORD run
to and fro throughout the whole earth,
to show himself strong in the behalf
of them whose heart is perfect toward him.
Herein thou hast done foolishly:
therefore from henceforth thou shalt have wars.
2 CHRONICLES 16:9

God longs to bring strength into your life if you will let Him. Obedience to God will bring this strength for daily living. Disobedience only brings trouble.

And he said, Hearken ye, all Judah,
and ye inhabitants of Jerusalem,
and thou king Jehoshaphat,
Thus saith the LORD unto you,
Be not afraid nor dismayed by
reason of this great multitude;
for the battle is not yours,
but God's.
2 CHRONICLES 20:15

Give that battle to the Lord. He will give you the victory.

But when he was strong,
his heart was lifted up to his destruction:
for he transgressed against the LORD his God,
and went into the temple of the LORD to
burn incense upon the altar of incense.
2 CHRONICLES 26:16

Uzziah was blessed by God until pride took hold of his heart. Don't let pride ruin your walk with God.

For the LORD brought Judah low
because of Ahaz king of Israel;
for he made Judah naked,
and transgressed sore
against the LORD.
2 CHRONICLES 28:19

All leaders have a tremendous responsibility and all of us are leaders in one capacity or another. Does your life reflect moral decline or integrity? Remember: Your life affects others.

———

And be not ye like your fathers,
and like your brethren,
which trespassed against
the LORD God of their fathers,
who therefore gave them up to desolation,
as ye see.
2 CHRONICLES 30:7

It may be up to the younger generation to bring us back to God. Young adults, stand up and be counted for the Lord. We need you.

And in every work that he began
in the service of the house of God,
and in the law,
and in the commandments,
to seek his God,
he did it with all his heart,
and prospered.
2 CHRONICLES 31:21

The Lord is still looking for people who will serve Him wholeheartedly. Can He count on you?

~∽~

With him is an arm of flesh;
but with us is the LORD our God to help us,
and to fight our battles.
And the people rested themselves upon
the words of Hezekiah king of Judah.
2 CHRONICLES 32:8

Dear child of God, you're not alone. God is on your side. The Lord can help you face any enemy. Claim the victory in the name of the Lord.

Because thine heart was tender,
and thou didst humble thyself before God,
when thou heardest his words against this place,
and against the inhabitants thereof,
and humbledst thyself before me,
and didst rend thy clothes,
and weep before me;
I have even heard thee also,
saith the LORD.
2 CHRONICLES 34:27

We must humble ourselves before God if we are
to be heard by God.

Ezra

Now in the first year of Cyrus king of Persia,
that the word of the LORD by
the mouth of Jeremiah might be fulfilled,
the LORD stirred up the spirit of
Cyrus king of Persia,
that he made a proclamation.
EZRA 1:1

God keeps His word. Be patient.

———

Thus saith Cyrus king of Persia,
The LORD God of heaven. . .
hath charged me to build him
an house at Jerusalem, which is in Judah.
EZRA 1:2

If God used a pagan king to see that the temple was rebuilt, you can put your trust in Him.

And some of the chief of the fathers,
when they came to the house of the LORD
which is at Jerusalem,
offered freely for the house of God
to set it up in his place.
EZRA 2:68

Joyful giving is a characteristic of those who love the Lord. Please note that the spiritual leaders lead the way. Are you setting a good example? Are you giving with a grateful heart?

———

And they sang together by course in praising
and giving thanks unto the LORD;
because he is good,
for his mercy endureth for ever toward Israel.
And all the people shouted with a great shout,
when they praised the LORD,
because the foundation of the house
of the LORD was laid.
EZRA 3:11

It's a good thing to worship the Lord. Attend worship services this week. It will lift your spirit.

Then the people of the land weakened
the hands of the people of Judah,
and troubled them in building.
EZRA 4:4

There will be those who seek to discourage you.
Keep going for the Lord. He will take care of you.

———

For Ezra had prepared his heart
to seek the law of the LORD,
and to do it,
and to teach in Israel
statutes and judgments.
EZRA 7:10

Are you daily preparing your heart to seek the
Lord? Involve Him in all areas of your life.

So we fasted and besought our God for this:
and he was entreated of us.
EZRA 8:23

God answers the prayers of those who seek Him.
His answer is always the best answer.

> *Now when Ezra had prayed,*
> *and when he had confessed,*
> *weeping and casting himself down*
> *before the house of God,*
> *there assembled unto him*
> *out of Israel a very great congregation*
> *of men and women and children:*
> *for the people wept very sore.*
> EZRA 10:1

Oh, that we would fall on our faces before God in confession and repentance! If we did, God would heal our broken hearts. He's ready. . .are we?

Nehemiah

But when Sanballat. . .and Tobiah. . .
and Geshem. . .heard it,
they laughed us to scorn, and despised us,
and said, What is this thing that ye do?
NEHEMIAH 2:19

There will always be those who make fun of people who seek to serve the Lord. That's to be expected. Don't give up. Keep going for the Lord.

———

So built we the wall;
and all the wall was joined together
unto the half thereof:
for the people had a mind to work.
NEHEMIAH 4:6

If God's people will work together for the Lord, wonderful things will happen.

And I looked, and rose up,
and said unto the nobles,
and to the rulers,
and to the rest of the people,
Be not ye afraid of them:
remember the Lord,
which is great and terrible,
and fight for your brethren,
your sons, and your daughters,
your wives, and your houses.
NEHEMIAH 4:14

"Remember the Lord." What great advice. Don't be afraid of what you face. Remember the Lord. He is the Prince of Peace.

And I sent messengers unto them, saying,
I am doing a great work,
so that I cannot come down:
why should the work cease,
whilst I leave it, and come down to you?
NEHEMIAH 6:3

Don't let a sinful world and its fleeting pleasures take you away from the high calling of God. Keep your eyes on the Lord.

That I gave my brother Hanani,
and Hananiah the ruler of the palace,
charge over Jerusalem:
for he was a faithful man,
and feared God above many.
NEHEMIAH 7:2

Can the Lord count on you? Be a man or woman of faith and integrity.

———

And Ezra opened the book in the sight of
all the people;
(for he was above all the people;)
and when he opened it,
all the people stood up:
And Ezra blessed the LORD,
the great God. And all the people answered,
Amen, Amen, with lifting up their hands:
and they bowed their heads,
and worshipped the LORD
with their faces to the ground.
NEHEMIAH 8:5–6

What would happen if everyone worshiped the Lord on a regular basis? This would be a much better world.

Then he said unto them,
Go your way,
eat the fat, and drink the sweet,
and send portions unto them
for whom nothing is prepared:
for this day is holy unto our Lord:
neither be ye sorry;
for the joy of the LORD is your strength.
NEHEMIAH 8:10

Are you weak and worn by the circumstances of your life? Look to the Lord, and watch His joy become your strength.

———

And they stood up in their place,
and read in the book of the law of the LORD
their God one fourth part of the day;
and another fourth part they confessed,
and worshipped the LORD their God.
NEHEMIAH 9:3

We, too, must take time to worship the Lord. Worship is great medicine for the soul.

Thou, even thou, art LORD alone;
thou hast made heaven,
the heaven of heavens,
with all their host, the earth,
and all things that are therein,
the seas, and all that is therein,
and thou preservest them all;
and the host of heaven worshippeth thee.
NEHEMIAH 9:6

This verse should be on the hearts of all who know and love the Lord. Worship the Lord. Rejoice that He is in control.

———

Howbeit thou art just in all
that is brought upon us;
for thou hast done right,
but we have done wickedly.
NEHEMIAH 9:33

You can count on the Lord always to do what is right. Also, don't forget His mercy and grace. He is the God who will forgive. Trust Him with your life.

Also that day they offered great sacrifices,
and rejoiced:
for God had made them rejoice with great joy:
the wives also and the children rejoiced:
so that the joy of Jerusalem
was heard even afar off.
NEHEMIAH 12:43

Real joy comes by giving back to God what rightfully belongs to Him. Give Him your best and experience the joy that only He can give.

Esther

For if thou altogether holdest
thy peace at this time,
then shall there enlargement and
deliverance arise to the Jews
from another place;
but thou and thy father's house
shall be destroyed:
and who knoweth whether
thou art come to the kingdom
for such a time as this?
ESTHER 4:14

It is not coincidence that God has placed you where you are. Now let Him use you. Remember, other lives will be affected and influenced by your decisions.

Job

There was a man in the land of Uz,
whose name was Job;
and that man was perfect and upright,
and one that feared God, and eschewed evil.
JOB 1:1

We need more men of Job's noble character. Will you be one?

———∿∿∿———

Naked came I out of my mother's womb,
and naked shall I return thither: the LORD gave,
and the LORD hath taken away;
blessed be the name of the LORD.
JOB 1:21

Job knew that he was ultimately in God's hands. All of us are accountable to God.

Behold, happy is the man
whom God correcteth:
therefore despise not thou
the chastening of the Almighty.
JOB 5:17

It's a privilege to experience God's correction in our lives. He works only for our good and His glory. Despise not the chastening of the Lord.

——•——

Man that is born of a woman is of few days,
and full of trouble.
JOB 14:1

Life is a gift. Life is short. Live it for the glory of God.

——•——

If a man die, shall he live again?
all the days of my appointed time will I wait,
till my change come.
JOB 14:14

Jesus answered this question in John 11:25: "I am the resurrection, and the life: he that believeth in me, though he were dead, yet shall he live."

For I know that my redeemer liveth,
and that he shall stand at
the latter day upon the earth:
And though after my skin
worms destroy this body,
yet in my flesh shall I see God.
JOB 19:25–26

I praise God that my Redeemer lives. Do you know Him? He loves you.

———

But he knoweth the way that I take:
when he hath tried me, I shall come forth as gold.
JOB 23:10

Times may be tough, but remember God is building your character and you shall come forth as gold.

———

I made a covenant with mine eyes;
why then should I think upon a maid?
JOB 31:1

What wholesome wisdom this is for all men! Devote your heart completely to the wife God has given you. Ask the Lord to help you keep such a covenant.

Did not he that made me
in the womb make him?
and did not one fashion us
in the womb?
JOB 31:15

Don't look down on others. God created them, too. He loves them and He loves you.

———

And the LORD turned
the captivity of Job,
when he prayed for his friends:
also the LORD gave
Job twice as much
as he had before.
JOB 42:10

God will take care of us if we are careful to pray for the needs of others. "But seek ye first the kingdom of God, and his righteousness; and all these things shall be added unto you" (Matthew 6:33).

Psalms

Blessed is the man that walketh
not in the counsel of the ungodly. . . .
But his delight is in the law of the LORD;
and in his law doth he meditate day and night.
PSALM 1:1–2

The word *blessed* can be translated as "happy."
With that in mind, try what these verses suggest
and you'll find the way to true happiness.

———

And he shall be like a tree planted
by the rivers of water,
that bringeth forth his fruit in his season.
PSALM 1:3

A man of God is a stable influence in an unstable
world. God will take care of those who walk with
Him.

I laid me down and slept;
I awaked; for the LORD sustained me.
PSALM 3:5

You can rest well when you know the Lord is with you. He is the One who gives peace that passes all understanding.

⸻

I will both lay me down in peace, and sleep:
for thou, LORD,
only makest me dwell in safety.
PSALM 4:8

You can sleep well when you're in God's hands. Do you have that kind of peace?

⸻

Behold, he travaileth with iniquity,
and hath conceived mischief,
and brought forth falsehood.
He made a pit, and digged it,
and is fallen into the ditch which he made.
PSALM 7:14–15

Troublemakers make the most trouble for themselves. Be a blessing, and experience blessing.

When I consider thy heavens,
the work of thy fingers,
the moon and the stars,
which thou hast ordained;
What is man,
that thou art mindful of him?
and the son of man,
that thou visitest him?
PSALM 8:3–4

Take time to consider the awesome creation of God and then consider that you are important to Him. Rejoice that our great God not only knows you but loves you, too. What a mighty God we serve!

———✽———

The wicked shall be turned into hell,
and all the nations that forget God.
PSALM 9:17

How many nations have learned this lesson the hard way? How many more still have not learned? "Lord, help us to bring honor to You."

The LORD is in his holy temple,
the LORD'S throne is in heaven:
his eyes behold, his eyelids try,
the children of men.
PSALM 11:4

No matter what happens, remember God is still on the throne! Remember also that He loves you.

—⁓—

The fool hath said in his heart,
There is no God. They are corrupt,
they have done abominable works,
there is none that doeth good.
PSALM 14:1

"In the beginning God created the heaven and the earth" (Genesis 1:1). God is and will always be.

—⁓—

I have set the LORD always before me:
because he is at my right hand,
I shall not be moved.
PSALM 16:8

Are you looking for stability? Make the Lord the focus of your life.

The heavens declare the glory of God;
and the firmament showeth his handiwork.
PSALM 19:1

Look around you and enjoy God's marvelous creation. We serve a great and mighty God.

—⁂—

Let the words of my mouth,
and the meditation of my heart,
be acceptable in thy sight, O LORD,
my strength, and my redeemer.
PSALM 19:14

This should be the attitude of every follower of the Lord. Allow the Lord to be the master of your thoughts and speech.

—⁂—

Some trust in chariots, and some in horses:
but we will remember the name of
the LORD our God.
PSALM 20:7

Put your trust in the Lord and not in the things of this world. The Lord never changes. You can always count on Him.

The LORD is my shepherd;
I shall not want.
PSALM 23:1

When you let the Lord shepherd your life, you will be blessed.

—∞—

The LORD is my light and my salvation;
whom shall I fear?
the LORD is the strength of my life;
of whom shall I be afraid?
PSALM 27:1

We have tremendous confidence when our faith is firmly rooted in the Lord. Don't let fear and doubt take hold. Put your trust in the Lord.

—∞—

Wait on the LORD:
be of good courage,
and he shall strengthen thine heart:
wait, I say, on the LORD.
PSALM 27:14

Don't give up. God is on the throne. Look to Him. He loves you.

By the word of the LORD
were the heavens made;
and all the host of them by
the breath of his mouth.
For he spake,
and it was done;
he commanded,
and it stood fast.
PSALM 33:6, 9

We serve a great God. He is the Creator and Sustainer of all. He doesn't even break a sweat. He speaks and it is done. Praise God!

—∿—

The angel of the LORD encampeth
round about them that fear him,
and delivereth them.
PSALM 34:7

God not only provides but He protects. You're in good hands when you're in God's hands.

The young lions do lack, and suffer hunger:
*but they that seek the L*ORD
shall not want any good thing.
PSALM 34:10

God provides for His own. "But seek ye first the kingdom of God, and his righteousness; and all these things shall be added unto you" (Matthew 6:33).

---

*The righteous cry, and the L*ORD *heareth,*
and delivereth them out of all their troubles.
PSALM 34:17

Go ahead. Cry out to God. He loves you and He will help you.

---

*Delight thyself also in the L*ORD*;*
and he shall give thee the desires of thine heart.
PSALM 37:4

When you get your joy from the Lord, you'll have a great day. . .and many more.

I have been young, and now am old;
yet have I not seen the righteous forsaken,
nor his seed begging bread.
PSALM 37:25

God is faithful. He takes care of His own. "But my God shall supply all your need according to his riches in glory by Christ Jesus" (Philippians 4:19).

LORD, make me to know mine end,
and the measure of my days, what it is;
that I may know how frail I am.
PSALM 39:4

You're not going to live forever on this earth. God will help you to understand the brevity of life and how to handle the days you have.

And now, Lord, what wait I for?
my hope is in thee.
PSALM 39:7

Hope is a wonderful possession, especially when we put our hope in the Lord.

I waited patiently for the LORD;
and he inclined unto me, and heard my cry.
He brought me up also out of an horrible pit,
out of the miry clay, and set my feet upon a rock,
and established my goings.
PSALM 40:1–2

The Lord can do the same for you. Trust the Lord to lift you up from despair into hope.

———

God is our refuge and strength,
a very present help in trouble.
PSALM 46:1

You don't have to be afraid. Trust in the Lord. He will be your shelter and strength.

———

Against thee, thee only, have I sinned,
and done this evil in thy sight:
that thou mightest be justified when thou speakest,
and be clear when thou judgest.
PSALM 51:4

All sin is against God. This is why we desperately need His forgiveness.

Create in me a clean heart, O God;
and renew a right spirit within me.
PSALM 51:10

God can clean up your life, too, if you commit it to Him. "Therefore if any man be in Christ, he is a new creature: old things are passed away; behold, all things are become new" (2 Corinthians 5:17).

———

Cast thy burden upon the LORD,
and he shall sustain thee:
he shall never suffer the righteous to be moved.
PSALM 55:22

The Lord will ease your load. He will give you the strength you need. He loves you.

———

Give us help from trouble:
for vain is the help of man.
PSALM 60:11

What we need most in life is God's help and wisdom. He's the One who can really take care of us.

O thou that hearest prayer,
unto thee shall all flesh come.
PSALM 65:2

The Lord hears our prayers. "Call unto me, and I will answer thee, and show thee great and mighty things, which thou knowest not" (Jeremiah 33:3).

———

If I regard iniquity in my heart,
the Lord will not hear me.
PSALM 66:18

Sin in our hearts hinders our prayer life. Confess sin and keep the lines open to God.

———

A father of the fatherless,
and a judge of the widows,
is God in his holy habitation.
PSALM 68:5

The Lord specializes in helping the helpless.

Blessed be the Lord,
who daily loadeth us with benefits,
even the God of our salvation. Selah.
PSALM 68:19

God is so good! Take time to count your many blessings.

———∽∾∽———

For the LORD God is a sun and shield:
the LORD will give grace and glory:
no good thing will he withhold
from them that walk uprightly.
PSALM 84:11

God loves to bless those who love Him. Walk with God and experience life at its best.

———∽∾∽———

Wilt thou not revive us again:
that thy people may rejoice in thee?
PSALM 85:6

If we pray this prayer, God will answer. "Lord, send a revival and let it begin in me."

Give ear, O LORD,
unto my prayer;
and attend to the voice
of my supplications.
In the day of my trouble
I will call upon thee:
for thou wilt answer me.
PSALM 86:6–7

You've tried everything else. Now call on God. He will help you. He loves you.

I will sing of the mercies
of the LORD for ever:
with my mouth will I
make known thy faithfulness
to all generations.
PSALM 89:1

Let's declare our love and appreciation for God. Others need to know how wonderful He is. "Let the redeemed of the LORD say so, whom he hath redeemed from the hand of the enemy" (Psalm 107:2).

LORD, thou hast been our dwellingplace
in all generations.
Before the mountains were brought forth,
or ever thou hadst formed
the earth and the world,
even from everlasting to everlasting,
thou art God.
PSALM 90:1–2

It makes good sense to place our lives into the hands of Almighty God. He is the One who never changes. We can depend on Him.

He that dwelleth in
the secret place of the
most High shall abide under
the shadow of the Almighty.
I will say of the LORD,
He is my refuge and my fortress:
my God; in him will I trust.
PSALM 91:1–2

There is a shelter from the storms of life. Live under the protection of the mighty and loving Lord. He loves you.

He that planted the ear,
shall he not hear?
he that formed the eye,
shall he not see?
PSALM 94:9

What a great question. God created the ear and the eye. God does hear and God does see. Would He be pleased with what He hears and sees in you?

Enter into his gates
with thanksgiving,
and into his courts with praise:
be thankful unto him,
and bless his name.
For the LORD is good;
his mercy is everlasting;
and his truth endureth
to all generations.
PSALM 100:4–5

The Lord is worthy of all praise and thanksgiving. Take time to show that you love and appreciate Him.

Bless the LORD, O my soul:
and all that is within me,
bless his holy name.
Bless the LORD, O my soul,
and forget not all his benefits.
PSALM 103:1–2

Count your blessings in the Lord and you will want to praise Him.

―⚬⚬―

As far as the east is from the west,
so far hath he removed
our transgressions from us.
PSALM 103:12

Forgiveness from the Lord is wonderful. Confess your sins and repent. He will do a wonderful work in you.

―⚬⚬―

They soon forgat his works;
they waited not for his counsel.
PSALM 106:13

Don't be guilty of forgetting the Lord and all His blessings. Continue to thank Him daily.

Let the redeemed of the LORD say so,
whom he hath redeemed from
the hand of the enemy.
PSALM 107:2

Tell the world what the Lord means to you. Those who don't know Him need Him desperately.

———

He sent his word, and healed them,
and delivered them from their destructions.
PSALM 107:20

God's Word has a healing effect upon the human heart. Open the Bible and read it. It will do you good.

———

I love the LORD,
because he hath heard my voice
and my supplications.
Because he hath inclined his ear unto me,
therefore will I call upon him as long as I live.
PSALM 116:1–2

Call on the Lord and you'll love Him, too. You can depend on Him.

The LORD is on my side;
I will not fear:
what can man do unto me?
PSALM 118:6

Have faith in God. He is the One you can trust.

———

This is the day which
the LORD hath made;
we will rejoice and be glad in it.
PSALM 118:24

Every day is a gift from God. Make today a good one with God's help.

———

Thy word have I hid in mine heart,
that I might not sin against thee.
PSALM 119:11

This is one of the keys to victorious Christian living. Do you have God's Word in your heart?

For ever, O LORD,
thy word is settled in heaven.
PSALM 119:89

God's Word is not for sale or compromise. It stands forever.

———

Thy word is a lamp unto my feet,
and a light unto my path.
PSALM 119:105

Are you having trouble finding your way? Open your Bible and see what God has to say. He knows the way.

———

Except the LORD build the house,
they labour in vain that build it:
except the LORD keep the city,
the watchman waketh but in vain.
PSALM 127:1

True success in life comes when we build our lives upon the Lord and His ways. It can be frustrating if we don't.

If thou, LORD,
shouldest mark iniquities,
O Lord, who shall stand?
But there is forgiveness with thee,
that thou mayest be feared.
PSALM 130:3–4

Thank the Lord for His wonderful forgiveness.

———

O give thanks unto the LORD;
for he is good: for his mercy endureth for ever.
O give thanks unto the God of gods:
for his mercy endureth for ever.
PSALM 136:1–2

Take time to give thanks to God. It will honor Him and bring joy to your soul.

———

I will praise thee;
for I am fearfully and wonderfully made:
marvellous are thy works;
and that my soul knoweth right well.
PSALM 139:14

You are God's special creation. Rejoice that the Lord made you and be all that He wants you to be.

Search me, O God, and know my heart:
try me, and know my thoughts:
And see if there be any wicked way in me,
and lead me in the way everlasting.
PSALM 139:23–24

When was the last time you allowed the Lord to give you a spiritual evaluation?

———

Set a watch, O LORD,
before my mouth;
keep the door of my lips.
PSALM 141:3

Words can hurt or heal. Let the Lord be Lord of your conversation.

———

The LORD is gracious,
and full of compassion;
slow to anger,
and of great mercy.
PSALM 145:8

The Lord is not only great, but He is compassionate as well. Share your burdens with Him now.

Thou openest thine hand,
and satisfiest the desire of every living thing.
PSALM 145:16

God is not stingy. He loves to meet our needs. "But my God shall supply all your need according to his riches in glory by Christ Jesus" (Philippians 4:19).

He healeth the broken in heart,
and bindeth up their wounds.
PSALM 147:3

Let the Lord minister to the needs of your heart. He is the Great Physician.

He telleth the number of the stars;
he calleth them all by their names.
Great is our Lord, and of great power:
his understanding is infinite.
PSALM 147:4–5

If our God knows every star in the heavens, He can easily take care of us.

Proverbs

The fear of the LORD is
the beginning of knowledge:
but fools despise wisdom and instruction.
PROVERBS 1:7

Knowledge begins with a healthy respect for God. All truth comes from Him. Without Him life would be meaningless.

———

Trust in the LORD with all thine heart;
and lean not unto thine own understanding.
In all thy ways acknowledge him,
and he shall direct thy paths.
PROVERBS 3:5–6

Ultimate trust should be placed in God. He knows what is best for us.

Honour the LORD with thy substance,
and with the firstfruits
of all thine increase:
So shall thy barns be filled with plenty,
and thy presses shall burst
out with new wine.
PROVERBS 3:9–10

Honor the Lord with your possessions and He will take care of you. "Bring ye all the tithes into the storehouse. . .and prove me now herewith, saith the LORD of hosts, if I will not open you the windows of heaven, and pour you out a blessing, that there shall not be room enough to receive it" (Malachi 3:10).

My son, despise not the chastening of the LORD;
neither be weary of his correction:
For whom the LORD loveth he correcteth;
even as a father the son
in whom he delighteth.
PROVERBS 3:11–12

Correction is a part of God's love for His children. That's one of the ways we know we belong to Him.

He that walketh uprightly walketh surely:
but he that perverteth his ways
shall be known.
PROVERBS 10:9

God gives confidence and security to those who walk with Him. You'll never walk alone with the Lord in your life.

———

Hatred stirreth up strifes:
but love covereth all sins.
PROVERBS 10:12

Hatred destroys. Love heals.

———

An hypocrite with his mouth
destroyeth his neighbour:
but through knowledge
shall the just be delivered.
PROVERBS 11:9

Truth will win out despite the rumors of hypocrites. God keeps the final books.

He that trusteth in his riches shall fall:
but the righteous shall flourish as a branch.
PROVERBS 11:28

Trusting in money and things will let us down. Living for the Lord will give us real life. The choice is ours to make.

—∞—

There is that speaketh like
the piercings of a sword:
but the tongue of the wise is health.
PROVERBS 12:18

What do we sound like when we speak? Let's be encouragers.

—∞—

He that walketh with wise men shall be wise:
but a companion of fools shall be destroyed.
PROVERBS 13:20

Who are your companions? They have much to do with your values and the choices you make. Choose your friends wisely.

There is a way which seemeth right unto a man,
but the end thereof are the ways of death.
PROVERBS 14:12

Satan, the evil one, is a liar and deceiver. Follow him and you will be destroyed. Follow Jesus and you will be saved. "Jesus saith unto him, I am the way, the truth, and the life: no man cometh unto the Father, but by me" (John 14:6).

———

Righteousness exalteth a nation:
but sin is a reproach to any people.
PROVERBS 14:34

Under which category would God place our nation?

———

A soft answer turneth away wrath:
but grievous words stir up anger.
PROVERBS 15:1

We need more gentle answers in our world today. There is already too much hatred and anger.

> *Commit thy works unto the LORD,*
> *and thy thoughts shall be established.*
> PROVERBS 16:3

Find God's will and then do God's will. This is the key to fulfillment.

> *How much better is it to get wisdom than gold!*
> PROVERBS 16:16

Here is real wealth defined. Read the Bible and get wealthy.

> *Pride goeth before destruction,*
> *and an haughty spirit before a fall.*
> PROVERBS 16:18

Pride can knock you off your feet. Humility keeps you stable.

> *A friend loveth at all times,*
> *and a brother is born for adversity.*
> PROVERBS 17:17

Be a real friend. Love others through the good times and the bad.

The words of a talebearer are as wounds,
and they go down into the innermost parts
of the belly.
PROVERBS 18:8

Don't be a gossip. Weigh your words carefully so that they may be a blessing.

———

Chasten thy son while there is hope,
and let not thy soul spare for his crying.
PROVERBS 19:18

Discipline is the work of loving parents. The lives of your children are at stake.

———

Wine is a mocker, strong drink is raging:
and whosoever is deceived thereby is not wise.
PROVERBS 20:1

Be wise and keep your life free from alcoholic beverages. These "mockers" truly destroy homes, jobs, and lives.

Train up a child in the way he should go:
and when he is old,
he will not depart from it.
PROVERBS 22:6

This is one of God's wonderful promises. Take time to show your child the way of the Lord. It will pay great dividends.

Foolishness is bound in the heart of a child;
but the rod of correction
shall drive it far from him.
PROVERBS 22:15

Loving discipline is a must for children. Parents, let's do what's right.

Hearken unto thy father that begat thee,
and despise not thy mother when she is old.
PROVERBS 23:22

Respect for parents is not only a blessing to both child and parents, but it is also a cornerstone for a righteous society.

Confidence in an unfaithful man
in time of trouble is like a broken tooth,
and a foot out of joint.
PROVERBS 25:19

Can people depend on you, or are you like a bad tooth that hurts all the time? God is looking for folks to be faithful to Him and to others.

———

Whoso diggeth a pit shall fall therein:
and he that rolleth a stone,
it will return upon him.
PROVERBS 26:27

If you're planning to make trouble for someone else, you might want to consider this verse. Sin pays bad dividends.

———

Boast not thyself of to morrow;
for thou knowest not what
a day may bring forth.
PROVERBS 27:1

Don't put off your commitment to the Lord. There may not be a tomorrow.

Iron sharpeneth iron;
so a man sharpeneth the
countenance of his friend.
PROVERBS 27:17

A good and honest friend is one of the greatest blessings of life. Be a blessing to someone else. Good friends are hard to find.

He that covereth his sins shall not prosper:
but whoso confesseth and
forsaketh them shall have mercy.
PROVERBS 28:13

Covering up your sins will only frustrate you. Come clean before God and He will forgive. It's wonderful to be forgiven.

He, that being often reproved hardeneth his neck,
shall suddenly be destroyed,
and that without remedy.
PROVERBS 29:1

Even God's patience can wear thin. Treat seriously what He has said to your heart. It's for your own good.

Correct thy son, and he shall give thee rest;
yea, he shall give delight unto thy soul.
PROVERBS 29:17

Discipline is first learned in the home. Parents, we have a heavy responsibility. Take time to love and discipline your children.

—⁓—

Who can find a virtuous woman?
for her price is far above rubies.
Her children arise up, and call her blessed;
her husband also, and he praiseth her.
Favour is deceitful, and beauty is vain:
but a woman that feareth the LORD,
she shall be praised.
PROVERBS 31:10, 28, 30

A woman of God has different priorities from many women today. She is concerned more about her inner beauty because she knows that pleases God.

Ecclesiastes

To every thing there is a season,
and a time to every purpose under the heaven.
ECCLESIASTES 3:1

Your life is no series of coincidences. It has a meaning and a purpose. God has a wonderful plan for you.

I know that, whatsoever God doeth,
it shall be for ever: nothing can be put to it,
nor any thing taken from it: and God doeth it,
that men should fear before him.
ECCLESIASTES 3:14

Believe it or not, the world does not revolve around you and me. God is in charge. Life takes on real meaning only when we are rightly related to Him. Get in touch with Him today.

Be not rash with thy mouth,
and let not thine heart be hasty
to utter any thing before God:
for God is in heaven, and thou upon earth:
therefore let thy words be few.
ECCLESIASTES 5:2

The fewer the words, the better. Think before you speak. God is listening.

———✦———

He that loveth silver shall not be
satisfied with silver;
nor he that loveth abundance with increase:
this is also vanity.
ECCLESIASTES 5:10

Material things will never satisfy the hunger of the soul. Only God can do that.

———✦———

As he came forth of his mother's womb,
naked shall he return to go as he came,
and shall take nothing of his labour,
which he may carry away in his hand.
ECCLESIASTES 5:15

What is important in life is not what we accumulate. . .but whom we glorify.

Better is the end of a thing
than the beginning thereof:
and the patient in spirit is
better than the proud in spirit.
ECCLESIASTES 7:8

Don't quit on God. Finish the race. Complete the course. Remember, the end—heaven—is better than the beginning.

———

Whatsoever thy hand findeth to do,
do it with thy might;
for there is no work, nor device,
nor knowledge, nor wisdom,
in the grave, whither thou goest.
ECCLESIASTES 9:10

Make the most of today. It is a gift from God. None of us has a promise of tomorrow.

———

The words of wise men are heard in quiet more
than the cry of him that ruleth among fools.
ECCLESIASTES 9:17

The loudest voices you hear may not be the wisest. Listen carefully to the advice you receive.

Remember now thy Creator
in the days of thy youth,
while the evil days come not,
nor the years draw nigh,
when thou shalt say,
I have no pleasure in them.
ECCLESIASTES 12:1

Young people, life becomes meaningful when you walk with God. Don't leave God out of your life.

—∾—

Let us hear the conclusion of the whole matter:
Fear God, and keep his commandments:
for this is the whole duty of man.
ECCLESIASTES 12:13

Meaningful life is found in fearing and obeying God. Our present and future existence depends on what we do with Jesus. Commit your all to Him.

Song of Solomon

He brought me to the banqueting house,
and his banner over me was love.
Song of Solomon 2:4

This biblical love story points us to the love and provision of God for His people.

───✺───

Set me as a seal upon thine heart,
as a seal upon thine arm:
for love is strong as death;
jealousy is cruel as the grave:
the coals thereof are coals of fire,
which hath a most vehement flame.
Song of Solomon 8:6

Don't underestimate the power of love and the cruelty of jealousy. Let love rule your heart.

Isaiah

Though your sins be as scarlet,
they shall be as white as snow;
though they be red like crimson,
they shall be as wool.
Isaiah 1:18

The Lord can remove the sin and guilt from your life. He loves you.

———∽∽∽———

And the loftiness of man shall be bowed down,
and the haughtiness of men shall be made low:
and the Lord alone shall be exalted in that day.
Isaiah 2:17

There is coming a day when everyone will acknowledge that the Lord is God and there is no other.

Woe unto them that rise up early in the morning,
that they may follow strong drink;
that continue until night, till wine inflame them!
ISAIAH 5:11

Destruction is the end for all who turn to alcohol for their answers or amusement.

———∽∾∽———

Woe unto them that call evil good, and good evil;
that put darkness for light, and light for darkness;
that put bitter for sweet, and sweet for bitter!
ISAIAH 5:20

Calling wrong right does not make it so. God has already set the standards for right and wrong. Our responsibility is to obey.

———∽∾∽———

Therefore the Lord himself shall give you a sign;
Behold, a virgin shall conceive,
and bear a son,
and shall call his name Immanuel.
ISAIAH 7:14

The virgin birth of the Savior was predicted by Isaiah seven hundred years before it took place. You can trust God to keep His word.

For unto us a child is born,
unto us a son is given:
and the government shall be upon his shoulder:
and his name shall be called
Wonderful, Counsellor, The mighty God,
The everlasting Father,
The Prince of Peace.
ISAIAH 9:6

Jesus fulfilled this promise. He is still Wonderful, Counselor, the mighty God, the Everlasting Father, and Prince of Peace.

———

How art thou fallen from heaven,
O Lucifer, son of the morning!
how art thou cut down to the ground,
which didst weaken the nations!
For thou hast said in thine heart,
I will ascend into heaven,
I will exalt my throne above the stars of God:
I will sit also upon the mount of the congregation,
in the sides of the north.
ISAIAH 14:12–13

People are most like the devil when "I" and "pride" are the focus of their lives.

For the LORD of hosts hath purposed,
and who shall disannul it?
ISAIAH 14:27

God's purposes will be accomplished. Don't find yourself in opposition to God's plans. Align your plans to fit His purposes.

———

Thou wilt keep him in perfect peace,
whose mind is stayed on thee:
because he trusteth in thee.
ISAIAH 26:3

Peace is yours if you focus on the Lord. Take time to read your Bible and pray. Then watch the Lord keep His promises.

———

Wherefore the Lord said,
Forasmuch as this people draw
near me with their mouth,
and with their lips do honour me,
but have removed their heart far from me. . . .
ISAIAH 29:13

Is your religion just lip service or is it from the heart? Serve the Lord with all your life.

Surely your turning of things
upside down shall be
esteemed as the potter's clay:
for shall the work say
of him that made it,
He made me not?
or shall the thing framed say of him
that framed it,
He had no understanding?
ISAIAH 29:16

Isn't it amazing how we turn the truth upside down? Here's the truth: This is God's world. He made it and He made you. That's the way it is.

The grass withereth,
the flower fadeth:
but the word of our God
shall stand for ever.
ISAIAH 40:8

The Word of God stands forever. You can trust God to keep His Word.

But they that wait upon the LORD
shall renew their strength;
they shall mount up with wings as eagles;
they shall run, and not be weary;
and they shall walk,
and not faint.
ISAIAH 40:31

Seeking the Lord has great benefits. The Lord can give you the strength you need. Lean on Him and watch the wonderful power work in you.

—∿—

Fear thou not; for I am with thee:
be not dismayed;
for I am thy God:
I will strengthen thee;
yea, I will help thee;
yea, I will uphold thee with
the right hand of my righteousness.
ISAIAH 41:10

The Lord is bigger than any fear or disappointment you face. He loves you. Let go and let God win the battles you face.

Look unto me, and be ye saved,
all the ends of the earth:
for I am God,
and there is none else.
ISAIAH 45:22

This invitation from the Lord is for you, too. Give your life to Him and be saved from your sins.

———

Surely he hath borne our griefs,
and carried our sorrows:
yet we did esteem him stricken,
smitten of God, and afflicted.
But he was wounded for our transgressions,
he was bruised for our iniquities:
the chastisement of our peace was upon him;
and with his stripes we are healed.
All we like sheep have gone astray;
we have turned every one to his own way;
and the LORD hath laid on him
the iniquity of us all.
ISAIAH 53:4–6

"Thank You, Jesus, for what You did for us on the cross. We will never forget Your great love for us."

Seek ye the LORD while he may be found,
call ye upon him while he is near.
ISAIAH 55:6

If God is speaking to your heart, don't take it for granted. Act now. It's a privilege that He has spoken to you.

———

Let the wicked forsake his way,
and the unrighteous man his thoughts:
and let him return unto the LORD,
and he will have mercy upon him;
and to our God, for he will abundantly pardon.
ISAIAH 55:7

The Lord will forgive if we repent. Take God at His Word today.

———

For as the heavens are higher than the earth,
so are my ways higher than your ways,
and my thoughts than your thoughts.
ISAIAH 55:9

To know and serve the Lord we must first take time to get alone with Him. Prayer and Bible study have great rewards.

Jeremiah

Before I formed thee in the belly I knew thee;
and before thou camest forth
out of the womb I sanctified thee,
and I ordained thee a prophet unto the nations.
JEREMIAH 1:5

Life is sacred. It is a gift from God. We must pray that from the womb to the tomb life will be honored and protected.

———∞———

Thus saith the LORD,
What iniquity have your fathers found in me,
that they are gone far from me,
and have walked after vanity?
JEREMIAH 2:5

How could we not love and serve the Lord? He has been so good to us.

For my people have committed two evils;
they have forsaken me the fountain of living waters,
and hewed them out cisterns, broken cisterns,
that can hold no water.
JEREMIAH 2:13

Does this describe your life? Turn back to the Lord and receive the abundant life that only He gives.

———∞———

Thus saith the LORD,
Let not the wise man glory in his wisdom,
neither let the mighty man glory in his might,
let not the rich man glory in his riches:
But let him that glorieth glory in this,
that he understandeth and knoweth me,
that I am the LORD which
exercise lovingkindness,
judgment, and righteousness, in the earth:
for in these things I delight,
saith the LORD.
JEREMIAH 9:23–24

The greatest thrill in life is to know the Lord. Do you know Him? He wants to be your Lord also.

Blessed is the man that trusteth in the LORD,
and whose hope the LORD is.
For he shall be as a tree planted by the waters,
and that spreadeth out her roots by the river,
and shall not see when heat cometh,
but her leaf shall be green;
and shall not be careful in the year of drought,
neither shall cease from yielding fruit.
JEREMIAH 17:7–8

Put your trust in the Lord. It will be a life of blessing and hope. He will also keep you strong in times of turmoil.

———

The heart is deceitful above all things,
and desperately wicked: who can know it?
JEREMIAH 17:9

Basically, humankind is not good. We are sinful. "For all have sinned, and come short of the glory of God" (Romans 3:23). This is why we need God's forgiveness of our sins. Have you asked the Lord to forgive you?

And ye shall seek me, and find me,
when ye shall search for me with all your heart.
JEREMIAH 29:13

If you're seriously seeking God you will find Him. That's a promise from God Himself.

—◦◦◦—

Ah Lord GOD! behold,
thou hast made the heaven and the earth by thy
great power and stretched out arm,
and there is nothing too hard for thee.
Behold, I am the LORD,
the God of all flesh:
is there any thing too hard for me?
JEREMIAH 32:17, 27

God can handle your problems. Put them in His capable hands.

—◦◦◦—

Call unto me, and I will answer thee,
and show thee great and mighty things,
which thou knowest not.
JEREMIAH 33:3

The Lord will do more than you could ever dream. Call unto Him. He loves you.

Lamentations

*It is of the LORD'S mercies that
we are not consumed,
because his compassions fail not.
They are new every morning:
great is thy faithfulness.*
LAMENTATIONS 3:22–23

Every day is a gift from God and should be treated with great care.

———∿∿∿———

*Turn thou us unto thee, O LORD,
and we shall be turned;
renew our days as of old.*
LAMENTATIONS 5:21

Have you been a drop-out for the cause of the Lord? Turn to Him. Let Him bring the blessings to your life like in the "old days." He can do it.

Ezekiel

When I say unto the wicked,
Thou shalt surely die;
and thou givest him not warning,
nor speakest to warn the wicked
from his wicked way, to save his life;
the same wicked man shall die in his iniquity,
but his blood will I require at thine hand.
EZEKIEL 3:18

Every follower of Christ has the responsibility to tell others about salvation. We cannot be secret disciples. The eternal destiny of souls is at stake.

———

I will recompense thee according to thy ways.
EZEKIEL 7:9

Don't trifle with God. He is the Judge of all humanity.

They shall cast their silver in the streets,
and their gold shall be removed:
their silver and their gold
shall not be able to
deliver them in the day of
the wrath of the LORD:
they shall not satisfy their souls,
neither fill their bowels:
because it is the stumblingblock
of their iniquity.
EZEKIEL 7:19

Money cannot buy peace of mind, nor can it fill the emptiness of the soul. Put your trust in God.

~~~

Therefore say unto the house of Israel,
Thus saith the Lord GOD;
Repent, and turn yourselves from your idols;
and turn away your faces from
all your abominations.
EZEKIEL 14:6

We need old-fashioned repentance of sin. What needs to be dealt with in your own life? Repent and experience God's forgiveness and cleansing.

For I have no pleasure in
the death of him that dieth,
saith the Lord GOD:
wherefore turn yourselves,
and live ye.
EZEKIEL 18:32

The Lord wants you to experience life at its best.
To do this, you must repent of your sins. Are you
willing to repent and live life at its best?

———

And they come unto thee
as the people cometh,
and they sit before thee as my people,
and they hear thy words,
but they will not do them:
for with their mouth
they show much love,
but their heart goeth
after their covetousness.
EZEKIEL 33:31

Hearing is not the same as doing. Neither is saying the same as doing. God is not interested in
our empty promises. He wants people who will
live what they say.

A new heart also will I give you,
and a new spirit will I put within you:
and I will take away
the stony heart out of your flesh,
and I will give you an heart of flesh.
EZEKIEL 36:26

The Lord can make your heart tender, too. Let go and let God take control of your life.

———

Again he said unto me,
Prophesy upon these bones,
and say unto them,
O ye dry bones, hear the word of the LORD.
Thus saith the Lord GOD unto these bones;
Behold, I will cause breath to enter into you,
and ye shall live.
EZEKIEL 37:4–5

The Lord still specializes in turning empty lives into ones that are full of meaning and purpose. Everyone needs the Lord.

Daniel

*But Daniel purposed in his heart that
he would not defile himself with
the portion of the king's meat,
nor with the wine which he drank:
therefore he requested of the prince of
the eunuchs that he might not defile himself.*
DANIEL 1:8

Have we purposed in our hearts not to defile ourselves with things that do not please God? Let's be a holy people for the glory of God.

―∾∾―

*Our God whom we serve is able to
deliver us from the burning fiery furnace. . . .
But if not. . .we will not serve thy gods.*
DANIEL 3:17–18

This is real faith. Trust God no matter the results.

Lo, I see four men loose,
walking in the midst of the fire,
and they have no hurt;
and the form of the fourth
is like the Son of God.
DANIEL 3:25

When you go through fiery trials, don't forget that the Son of God will be with you. God loves you. Trust Him with your life.

———

I thought it good to
show the signs and wonders
that the high God hath wrought toward me.
DANIEL 4:2

It is good to tell others what the Lord has done in your life. Tell your family and your friends.

———

And at the end of the days I Nebuchadnezzar
lifted up mine eyes unto heaven,
and mine understanding returned unto me.
DANIEL 4:34

Lift your eyes toward heaven and you, too, will come to a better understanding about life and eternity.

*Now when Daniel knew that
the writing was signed,
he went into his house;
and his windows being open
in his chamber toward Jerusalem,
he kneeled upon his knees three times a day,
and prayed, and gave thanks before his God,
as he did aforetime.*
DANIEL 6:10

We need more Daniels today. Let's rise up and be men and women of prayer.

Hosea

My people are destroyed for lack of knowledge:
because thou hast rejected knowledge,
I will also reject thee. . .
seeing thou hast forgotten the law of thy God,
I will also forget thy children.
HOSEA 4:6

Don't reject God's plan for your life. Read the Bible and become better acquainted with the will of God. You'll be glad you did.

Though thou, Israel, play the harlot,
yet let not Judah offend. . .
neither go ye up to Bethaven, nor swear,
The LORD liveth.
HOSEA 4:15

Sometimes God withdraws His blessings so that He can get our attention about sin in our lives.

For I desired mercy,
and not sacrifice;
and the knowledge of God
more than burnt offerings.
HOSEA 6:6

The Lord is more interested in sincerity of love for Him than rituals. Have a genuine love for God.

———

For they have sown the wind,
and they shall reap the whirlwind:
it hath no stalk:
the bud shall yield no meal:
if so be it yield,
the strangers shall swallow it up.
HOSEA 8:7

When you sow sin in your life, you will reap heartache and destruction. God has a better plan. Love Him, and then live for Him.

Sow to yourselves in righteousness,
reap in mercy;
break up your fallow ground:
for it is time to seek the LORD,
till he come and
rain righteousness upon you.
HOSEA 10:12

Our world needs to turn to God now. We need a revival. Begin by seeking the Lord with all your heart.

———

Who is wise,
and he shall understand these things?
prudent, and he shall know them?
for the ways of the LORD are right,
and the just shall walk in them:
but the transgressors shall fall therein.
HOSEA 14:9

Are you wise and prudent? If you are, you will realize that God's way is the best way.

Joel

And rend your heart, and not your garments,
*and turn unto the L*ORD *your God:*
for he is gracious and merciful,
slow to anger, and of great kindness,
and repenteth him of the evil.
JOEL 2:13

God is ready to forgive if you are ready to repent of your sin.

And I will restore to you the years
that the locust hath eaten, the cankerworm,
and the caterpillar, and the palmerworm,
my great army which I sent among you.
JOEL 2:25

The Lord can make up for your wasted years. It's not too late to start serving the Lord.

And it shall come to pass afterward,
that I will pour out my spirit upon all flesh;
and your sons and your daughters shall prophesy,
your old men shall dream dreams,
your young men shall see visions.
JOEL 2:28

When God pours His spirit upon you, you'll know it. Ask God for a fresh touch so that you may be a person of faith and vision.

Amos

Therefore thus will I do unto thee, O Israel:
and because I will do this unto thee,
prepare to meet thy God, O Israel.
AMOS 4:12

Are you prepared to meet the Lord? You can be if you put your life in His hands. "And as it is appointed unto men once to die, but after this the judgment" (Hebrews 9:27).

For thus saith the LORD unto the house of Israel,
Seek ye me, and ye shall live.
AMOS 5:4

Real living occurs when we seek the Lord. Get on your knees, open your Bible, and seek the Lord now.

Behold, the days come, saith the Lord GOD,
that I will send a famine in the land,
not a famine of bread,
nor a thirst for water,
but of hearing the words of the LORD.
AMOS 8:11

Don't take the Bible for granted. Someday we may not have such easy access to God's Word.

Obadiah

The pride of thine heart hath deceived thee. . .
whose habitation is high; that saith in his heart,
Who shall bring me down to the ground?
OBADIAH 3

How many times have we deceived ourselves by putting our trust in our own foolish pride? "Humble yourselves therefore under the mighty hand of God, that he may exalt you in due time" (1 Peter 5:6).

For the day of the LORD
is near upon all the heathen:
as thou hast done, it shall be done unto thee.
OBADIAH 15

God is just. Therefore He must judge. Commit to Him now as your Lord and Savior.

Jonah

But Jonah rose up to flee unto Tarshish
from the presence of the LORD.
JONAH 1:3

Are you running from the Lord? You're only hurting yourself. Repent now and follow Him.

———

Now the LORD had prepared
a great fish to swallow up Jonah.
And Jonah was in the belly
of the fish three days and three nights.
JONAH 1:17

God has everything under control. A great fish was waiting for the rebellious prophet. You can't run away from the Lord.

Micah

Hear, all ye people;
hearken, O earth, and all that therein is:
and let the Lord GOD be witness against you.
MICAH 1:2

The Lord sees and knows all. He is a witness to our
every thought and deed. Is He pleased with us?

———

But thou, Bethlehem Ephratah,
though thou be little among
the thousands of Judah,
yet out of thee shall he come forth
unto me that is to be ruler in Israel.
MICAH 5:2

Hundreds of years before Jesus was born in Bethlehem, Micah predicted the blessed event. You
can depend on the Word of God.

He hath showed thee, O man, what is good;
and what doth the LORD require of thee,
but to do justly, and to love mercy,
and to walk humbly with thy God?
MICAH 6:8

Those of us who know the Lord should live holy lives. Can people tell we belong to Him?

———

Who is a God like unto thee,
that pardoneth iniquity,
and passeth by the transgression
of the remnant of his heritage?
he retaineth not his anger for ever,
because he delighteth in mercy.
MICAH 7:18

The Lord longs to pardon and forgive those who come to Him. Remember that He loves you.

Nahum

The LORD is slow to anger, and great in power,
and will not at all acquit the wicked:
the LORD hath his way in the whirlwind
and in the storm,
and the clouds are the dust of his feet.
NAHUM 1:3

Don't interpret the Lord's patience as weakness.
Get right with God today. Judgment will come to
those who don't love and obey Him.

The LORD is good,
a strong hold in the day of trouble;
and he knoweth them that trust in him.
NAHUM 1:7

Has life beat you down? Go to the Lord. He will
comfort and strengthen you.

Habakkuk

But the LORD is in his holy temple:
let all the earth keep silence before him.
HABAKKUK 2:20

If you feel loaded down with the cares of this world, don't forget that God is still on His throne. Be silent and take comfort in this glorious truth. He will take care of you.

O LORD, I have heard thy speech,
and was afraid: O LORD,
revive thy work in the midst of the years,
in the midst of the years make known;
in wrath remember mercy.
HABAKKUK 3:2

"Lord, this is my prayer for the sin-sick world. Lord, send a revival." Will you join me in prayer for the urgent need of revival?

Zephaniah

Neither their silver nor their gold shall be able
to deliver them in the day of the LORD'S wrath;
but the whole land shall be devoured by
the fire of his jealousy.
ZEPHANIAH 1:18

Money or influence cannot buy a reprieve from
God's judgment. Only a heart commitment to the
Lord can save us. Do you know the Lord?

———

The LORD. . .will rejoice over thee with joy;
he will rest in his love,
he will joy over thee with singing.
ZEPHANIAH 3:17

It's a blessing to belong to the Lord. He loves to
take care of His own. Are you His?

Haggai

Ye have sown much, and bring in little;
ye eat, but ye have not enough;
ye drink, but ye are not filled with drink. . . .
Thus saith the LORD of hosts;
Consider your ways.
HAGGAI 1:6–7

Are you missing something? Perhaps it's time for you to do a personal inventory. Consider your ways and your relationship with God.

The silver is mine, and the gold is mine,
saith the LORD of hosts.
HAGGAI 2:8

Remember that your possessions are only on loan from the Lord. We are His stewards. Be wise with what He gives you.

Zechariah

Therefore say thou unto them,
Thus saith the LORD of hosts;
Turn ye unto me, saith the LORD of hosts,
and I will turn unto you, saith the LORD of hosts.
ZECHARIAH 1:3

When we ask God to forgive us, He is eager to wipe the slate clean. "If we confess our sins, he is faithful and just to forgive us our sins, and to cleanse us from all unrighteousness" (1 John 1:9).

Then he answered and spake unto me, saying,
This is the word of the LORD unto Zerubbabel,
saying, Not by might, nor by power,
but by my spirit, saith the LORD of hosts.
ZECHARIAH 4:6

Nothing can accomplish what God's Spirit, the Holy Spirit, can, moving in us.

Malachi

A son honoureth his father,
and a servant his master:
if then I be a father, where is mine honour?
and if I be a master, where is my fear?
saith the LORD of hosts unto you.
MALACHI 1:6

Where is the respect for Almighty God? He is the Creator and Sustainer of the universe. He deserves our respect and obedience.

———

For the LORD, the God of Israel,
saith that he hateth putting away.
MALACHI 2:16

The Lord hates divorce because He knows the heartache it brings. Let the Lord be the foundation of your marriage. He can preserve it.

Bring ye all the tithes into the storehouse,
that there may be meat in mine house,
and prove me now herewith,
saith the LORD of hosts,
if I will not open you
the windows of heaven,
and pour you out a blessing,
that there shall not be
room enough to receive it.
MALACHI 3:10

God blesses the faithful who give back to Him. Try tithing, and you will see God blessing your life.

Matthew

And she shall bring forth a son,
and thou shalt call his name JESUS:
for he shall save his people from their sins.
MATTHEW 1:21

Before Jesus' birth an angel of the Lord told Joseph the reason Jesus was to come. Have you figured it out yet? He came to save you from your sins.

———

Where is he that is born King of the Jews?
for we have seen his star in the east,
and are come to worship him.
MATTHEW 2:2

The wise men had it right. Jesus is worthy to be worshiped. Let's follow their example. Let's give our best to Jesus.

But he answered and said,
It is written,
Man shall not live by bread alone,
but by every word that proceedeth
out of the mouth of God.
MATTHEW 4:4

Life is more than just existing in this material world. Real life is found in having a personal relationship with God.

———

Let your light so shine before men,
that they may see your good works,
and glorify your Father which is in heaven.
MATTHEW 5:16

Live for Jesus and your life will bring praise to the Lord. There are many in darkness who need the light of God to shine upon them.

———

But seek ye first the kingdom of God,
and his righteousness;
and all these things shall be added unto you.
MATTHEW 6:33

When we put God first, He takes care of our needs.

Enter ye in at the strait gate:
for wide is the gate, and broad is the way,
that leadeth to destruction,
and many there be which go in thereat:
Because strait is the gate, and narrow is the way,
which leadeth unto life,
and few there be that find it.
MATTHEW 7:13–14

The way to heaven is indeed narrow. "Neither is there salvation in any other: for there is none other name under heaven given among men, whereby we must be saved" (Acts 4:12). Are you on the right road? Do you know the only way to salvation?

And he saith unto them,
Why are ye fearful, O ye of little faith?
Then he arose, and rebuked the winds and the sea;
and there was a great calm.
But the men marvelled, saying,
What manner of man is this,
that even the winds and the sea obey him!
MATTHEW 8:26–27

Jesus can calm the storms of your life. He's more than a man. He is God the Son.

And as Jesus passed forth from thence,
he saw a man, named Matthew,
sitting at the receipt of custom:
and he saith unto him, Follow me.
And he arose, and followed him.
MATTHEW 9:9

Are you willing to follow Jesus wherever He leads? Matthew never regretted that decision and neither will you.

But when Jesus heard that,
he said unto them,
They that be whole need not a physician,
but they that are sick.
But go ye and learn what that meaneth,
I will have mercy, and not sacrifice:
for I am not come to call the righteous,
but sinners to repentance.
MATTHEW 9:12–13

Jesus can help us only when we realize we have a problem. He delights in helping the helpless.

Whosoever therefore shall confess me before men,
him will I confess also before my Father
which is in heaven.
MATTHEW 10:32

Real Christians are not ashamed to tell others about Jesus. What we declare on earth is declared in heaven.

———

Come unto me,
all ye that labour
and are heavy laden,
and I will give you rest.
Take my yoke upon you,
and learn of me;
for I am meek and lowly in heart:
and ye shall find rest unto your souls.
For my yoke is easy,
and my burden is light.
MATTHEW 11:28–30

This is a personal invitation from Jesus. How do you respond? Give your life to Him and experience life at its best.

> *He that is not with me*
> *is against me;*
> *and he that gathereth*
> *not with me scattereth abroad.*
> MATTHEW 12:30

Are you on the Lord's side? The odds are not good when you are against the Lord. There is no in-between with God.

> *Another parable spake he unto them;*
> *The kingdom of heaven is*
> *like unto leaven,*
> *which a woman took,*
> *and hid in three measures of meal,*
> *till the whole was leavened.*
> MATTHEW 13:33

God works His purposes through His people as they live and work in this world. Make a difference for the glory of God! Start today and see what just a little can do for the Kingdom of God.

And he said, Come.
And when Peter was come down out of the ship,
he walked on the water, to go to Jesus.
But when he saw the wind boisterous,
he was afraid; and beginning to sink,
he cried, saying, Lord, save me.
MATTHEW 14:29–30

Jesus is still in the saving business. If you're drowning in grief, fear, depression, or doubt, turn to Jesus. He will lift you out of the waves of despair.

He saith unto them,
But whom say ye that I am?
And Simon Peter answered and said,
Thou art the Christ,
the Son of the living God.
MATTHEW 16:15–16

Jesus was not just a good man. He is the Christ, the Son of the living God. Do you know the Jesus of the Bible?

While he yet spake, behold,
a bright cloud overshadowed them:
and behold a voice out of the cloud,
which said, This is my beloved Son,
in whom I am well pleased;
hear ye him.
MATTHEW 17:5

We need to heed the advice of our Heavenly Father. Listen to Jesus. Obey Him. Obedience will bless not only ourselves but others also.

———

But whoso shall offend one of
these little ones which believe in me,
it were better for him that a millstone
were hanged about his neck,
and that he were drowned
in the depth of the sea.
MATTHEW 18:6

If you're a stumbling block for children to come to Jesus, you're in trouble. Let your children see Jesus in you.

He saith unto them,
Moses because of the hardness of your hearts
suffered you to put away your wives:
but from the beginning it was not so.
MATTHEW 19:8

It's time we recognize the devastation of divorce on society. Let's allow Jesus' love to fill our homes. He has the power to make marriages happy and lasting.

But it shall not be so among you:
but whosoever will be great among you,
let him be your minister;
And whosoever will be chief among you,
let him be your servant:
Even as the Son of man
came not to be ministered unto,
but to minister,
and to give his life a ransom for many.
MATTHEW 20:26–28

True greatness is found in serving the Lord and others. Look at the life of Jesus and see this truth come to life.

Master, which is the great
commandment in the law?
Jesus said unto him,
Thou shalt love the Lord thy God
with all thy heart,
and with all thy soul, and with all thy mind.
This is the first and great commandment.
And the second is like unto it,
Thou shalt love thy neighbour as thyself.
On these two commandments hang
all the law and the prophets.
MATTHEW 22:36–40

These words sum up Christianity. Let's be real for Jesus. Let's love the Lord and others. What a great testimony we live when we live a life of love for the glory of God.

———

But he that is greatest among you
shall be your servant.
MATTHEW 23:11

Do you really want to be great? Be a servant. Share Christ's love with encouraging words and acts of love.

Heaven and earth shall pass away,
but my words shall not pass away.
MATTHEW 24:35

You can depend on God and His Word. He always keeps His promises.

———

Watch therefore,
for ye know neither the day nor
the hour wherein the Son of man cometh.
MATTHEW 25:13

Jesus is coming back. Are you ready? Commit your life to Jesus before it's too late.

———

Watch and pray,
that ye enter not into temptation:
the spirit indeed is willing,
but the flesh is weak.
MATTHEW 26:41

Do not neglect prayer. You need it to face temptations.

Now when the centurion,
and they that were with him,
watching Jesus, saw the earthquake,
and those things that were done,
they feared greatly, saying,
Truly this was the Son of God.
MATTHEW 27:54

Have you made the wonderful discovery that Jesus is the Son of God? Pray and ask God to reveal this truth to you.

———

He is not here:
for he is risen, as he said.
Come, see the place where the Lord lay.
MATTHEW 28:6

Jesus is the risen Savior and Lord. Commit your life to Him.

Mark

And in the morning,
rising up a great while before day,
he went out,
and departed into a solitary place,
and there prayed.
MARK 1:35

There is no substitute for a quiet time with God. If Jesus felt the need, consider how important quiet time is for us.

———

And they come unto him,
bringing one sick of the palsy,
which was borne of four.
MARK 2:3

Whom have you brought to Jesus lately?

> *For whosoever shall do the will of God,*
> *the same is my brother,*
> *and my sister, and mother.*
> MARK 3:35

Obedience to the Lord is one of the best indicators of our relationship to Him. Christians, do our actions match our words?

―∿―

> *And he arose, and rebuked the wind,*
> *and said unto the sea,*
> *Peace, be still.*
> *And the wind ceased,*
> *and there was a great calm.*
> MARK 4:39

Let Jesus bring peace to the storms of your life. He can do it.

―∿―

> *As soon as Jesus heard the word that was spoken,*
> *he saith unto the ruler of the synagogue,*
> *Be not afraid, only believe.*
> MARK 5:36

Jesus can replace fear with faith. Cast your cares upon Him.

And they went out,
and preached that men should repent.
MARK 6:12

Repentance is an important part of the Gospel message. Jesus came to save us from our sins, not in our sins.

———

He hath done all things well:
he maketh both the deaf to hear,
and the dumb to speak.
MARK 7:37

Jesus does all things well. Commit your ways to Him.

———

Jesus said unto him, If thou canst believe,
all things are possible to him that believeth.
And straightway the father of the child cried out,
and said with tears, Lord, I believe;
help thou mine unbelief.
MARK 9:23–24

If we cry out to the Lord for more faith, He is always faithful. We serve a great God.

What therefore God hath joined together,
let not man put asunder.
MARK 10:9

Marriage is not to be taken lightly. Commit yourself to your spouse for a lifetime.

———

And he taught, saying unto them,
Is it not written,
My house shall be called of
all nations the house of prayer?
but ye have made it a den of thieves.
MARK 11:17

God's people must pray. Prayer is a wonderful source of wisdom and power.

———

And when ye stand praying, forgive,
if ye have ought against any:
that your Father also which is in heaven
may forgive you your trespasses.
MARK 11:25

An unforgiving attitude is a barrier that can stand between us and a vital relationship with Jesus. Let it go. You will feel so much better.

And as touching the dead, that they rise:
have ye not read in the book of Moses,
how in the bush God spake unto him,
saying, I am the God of Abraham,
and the God of Isaac, and the God of Jacob?
He is not the God of the dead,
but the God of the living:
ye therefore do greatly err.
MARK 12:26–27

Our Lord specializes in life abundant and life eternal. Do you know Him? He is the very source of life, love, and fulfillment.

———

And Peter followed him afar off,
even into the palace of the high priest:
and he sat with the servants,
and warmed himself at the fire.
MARK 14:54

When we follow Jesus from a distance we are apt, like Peter, to have problems. Let's walk hand in hand with our Lord.

And so Pilate,
willing to content the people,
released Barabbas unto them,
and delivered Jesus,
when he had scourged him,
to be crucified.
MARK 15:15

Are we like Pilate? Are we trying to please the crowd instead of God? Our world needs people who will unashamedly stand up for Jesus. Will you be one?

Luke

For with God nothing shall be impossible.
LUKE 1:37

God can handle your problems. Give them to Him.

—◆—

And he came to Nazareth,
where he had been brought up:
and, as his custom was,
he went into the synagogue on the sabbath day,
and stood up for to read.
LUKE 4:16

Is it your custom to go to God's house? Be faithful in worship attendance. You'll be glad you went.

When Simon Peter saw it,
he fell down at Jesus' knees, saying,
Depart from me;
for I am a sinful man,
O Lord.
LUKE 5:8

Here is a snapshot of humanity and deity. Man is sinful, but God is holy. We can be made right in God's eyes only by His grace poured upon us by His Son Jesus.

⸻

And the whole multitude
sought to touch him:
for there went virtue out of him,
and healed them all.
LUKE 6:19

Reach out to Jesus and let Him touch your life. Jesus specializes in healing broken lives. Don't put it off another day. Let Him make a difference in you now. You, too, will never be the same.

And he came and touched the bier:
and they that bare him stood still.
And he said, Young man,
I say unto thee, Arise.
And he that was dead sat up,
and began to speak.
And he delivered him to his mother.
LUKE 7:14–15

Jesus is still bringing life and hope to those who have none. Are you living in despair? Let Jesus touch you.

———

And they came to him, and awoke him,
saying, Master, master, we perish.
Then he arose,
and rebuked the wind and
the raging of the water:
and they ceased,
and there was a calm.
LUKE 8:24

Let Jesus calm the storms of your life. Put your circumstances into His capable hands.

For what is a man advantaged,
if he gain the whole world,
and lose himself, or be cast away?
LUKE 9:25

You can "have it all" and yet have nothing. The person who has it all is the one who knows Jesus. "The LORD is my shepherd; I shall not want" (Psalm 23:1).

———

Notwithstanding in this rejoice not,
that the spirits are subject unto you;
but rather rejoice,
because your names are written in heaven.
LUKE 10:20

There's joy in being used by God. But there's greater joy in knowing that we are saved and will spend eternity in heaven. Praise the Lord! By the way, do you know you're going to heaven? You can by committing your life to Jesus as Savior and Lord.

And I say unto you,
Ask, and it shall be given you;
seek, and ye shall find;
knock, and it shall be opened unto you.
For every one that asketh receiveth;
and he that seeketh findeth;
and to him that knocketh
it shall be opened.
LUKE 11:9–10

"Blessed are they which do hunger and thirst after righteousness: for they shall be filled" (Matthew 5:6). What a goal for our lives!

And he said unto them,
Take heed, and beware of covetousness:
for a man's life consisteth not in
the abundance of the things
which he possesseth.
LUKE 12:15

Owning things does not make life fulfilling. Things will rust out and wear out. Knowing and serving Jesus, however, will make life very fulfilling.

I tell you, Nay:
but, except ye repent,
ye shall all likewise perish.
LUKE 13:3

Repentance of sin is essential to salvation. Repentance is a 180 degree turn away from sin.

———

For whosoever exalteth himself shall be abased;
and he that humbleth himself shall be exalted.
LUKE 14:11

The Lord has the final say-so on greatness. "Humble yourselves in the sight of the Lord, and he shall lift you up" (James 4:10).

———

I say unto you,
that likewise joy shall be in heaven
over one sinner that repenteth,
more than over ninety and nine just persons,
which need no repentance.
LUKE 15:7

Have you brought joy to heaven yet? You can by giving your life to Jesus. (At the same time, you'll bring great joy to your own heart.)

No servant can serve two masters:
for either he will hate the one,
and love the other;
or else he will hold to the one,
and despise the other.
Ye cannot serve God and mammon.
LUKE 16:13

It can't be any clearer than this! Who or what is your God?

And if he trespass against thee
seven times in a day,
and seven times in a day
turn again to thee,
saying, I repent;
thou shalt forgive him.
And the apostles said unto the Lord,
Increase our faith.
LUKE 17:4–5

Are you having trouble forgiving someone? Ask the Lord to increase your faith and forgiveness will come.

And he spake a parable unto them to this end,
that men ought always to pray,
and not to faint.
LUKE 18:1

Prayer is a must, not an option. Take time to pray.

———

For the Son of man is come to seek
and to save that which was lost.
LUKE 19:10

Jesus came because all of us need Him. "For all have sinned, and come short of the glory of God" (Romans 3:23). Give your life to Jesus.

———

For he is not a God of the dead,
but of the living: for all live unto him.
LUKE 20:38

Life abundant and life eternal come from the Lord. Let Jesus make your life all that it can be. Trust Him today.

And he said,
Of a truth I say unto you,
that this poor widow hath cast in
more than they all:
For all these have of their abundance cast
in unto the offerings of God:
but she of her penury
hath cast in all the living that she had.
LUKE 21:3–4

The Lord may be more interested in how much we kept for ourselves than in what we gave in the offering plate.

———

But ye shall not be so:
but he that is greatest among you,
let him be as the younger;
and he that is chief,
as he that doth serve.
LUKE 22:26

Servanthood is a sign of real greatness. Jesus set the example for all of us.

Then said Jesus, Father,
forgive them;
for they know not what they do.
And they parted his raiment,
and cast lots.
LUKE 23:34

It's in the heart of Jesus to forgive. Is it in your heart to repent?

He is not here, but is risen:
remember how he spake unto you
when he was yet in Galilee.
LUKE 24:6

Jesus is alive! He appeared to over five hundred people after He arose from the dead. He is Lord of all and He wants to be your Lord. He can make the difference in you for time and eternity. "Jesus Christ the same yesterday, and to day, and for ever" (Hebrews 13:8).

John

In the beginning was the Word,
and the Word was with God,
and the Word was God.
And the Word was made flesh,
and dwelt among us,
(and we beheld his glory,
the glory as of the
only begotten of the Father,)
full of grace and truth.
JOHN 1:1, 14

Jesus is God's Son who came to take away the sins of the world. By the way, He is the one and only Son of God. Also, He is the only way to heaven. Have you submitted your life to Him?

Jesus answered and said unto him,
Verily, verily, I say unto thee,
Except a man be born again,
he cannot see the kingdom of God.
JOHN 3:3

Being born again is not an option. It is a necessity for salvation.

—∞—

For God so loved the world,
that he gave his only begotten Son,
that whosoever believeth in him
should not perish, but have everlasting life.
JOHN 3:16

When Jesus died for the world, He died for you. Put your life in His hands.

—∞—

He that believeth on him is not condemned:
but he that believeth not is condemned already,
because he hath not believed in the name
of the only begotten Son of God.
JOHN 3:18

If you have not given your life to Jesus, you are already condemned to hell. Repent before it is too late.

Jesus answered and said unto her,
Whosoever drinketh of this water
shall thirst again:
But whosoever drinketh of the water
that I shall give him shall never thirst;
but the water that I shall give him
shall be in him a well of water
springing up into everlasting life.
JOHN 4:13–14

Is your life empty? Jesus gives life that satisfies abundantly. He will fill your life with love, joy, peace, and all the wonderful virtues of life.

———

But Jesus answered them,
My Father worketh hitherto,
and I work.
JOHN 5:17

God is always at work. When you find out what He is doing and join Him, life becomes very fulfilling. Don't put it off. Let your life count for Jesus.

And Jesus said unto them,
I am the bread of life:
he that cometh to me shall never hunger;
and he that believeth on me shall never thirst.
JOHN 6:35

Jesus can fill the emptiness of your life. Submit yourself to Him.

———

He that believeth on me,
as the scripture hath said,
out of his belly shall flow
rivers of living water.
JOHN 7:38

Your life will not be stagnant if you walk with Jesus. Let His life flow through you.

———

If the Son therefore shall make you free,
ye shall be free indeed.
JOHN 8:36

Jesus can set us free from the greatest slavery of all—the slavery of self.

The thief cometh not,
but for to steal, and to kill,
and to destroy:
I am come that they might have life,
and that they might
have it more abundantly.
JOHN 10:10

Accept no substitutes. Jesus is the One who gives real, abundant life.

Jesus said unto her,
I am the resurrection,
and the life:
he that believeth in me,
though he were dead,
yet shall he live.
JOHN 11:25

Dear Christians, you don't have to fear death. Jesus conquered death for you. If you haven't already come to Jesus, come now. "For whosoever shall call upon the name of the Lord shall be saved" (Romans 10:13).

And I, if I be lifted up from the earth,
will draw all men unto me.
JOHN 12:32

There's something wonderful and powerful about
the proclamation of Jesus as Savior and Lord. Is He
drawing you to Himself? When you surrender
your life to Him, you'll be forever glad you did.

———

A new commandment I give unto you,
That ye love one another;
as I have loved you,
that ye also love one another.
By this shall all men know
that ye are my disciples,
if ye have love one to another.
JOHN 13:34–35

Love for one another should be one way that people recognize Christians. This could be the greatest public relations and testimony to a world who
needs Jesus. Love your brothers and sisters in the
Lord.

Jesus saith unto him,
I am the way, the truth, and the life:
no man cometh unto the Father, but by me.
JOHN 14:6

The only way to heaven is through Jesus. Do you know Him?

———∞———

I am the vine, ye are the branches:
He that abideth in me, and I in him,
the same bringeth forth much fruit:
for without me ye can do nothing.
JOHN 15:5

We can do nothing without the Lord. He is our life and our all.

———∞———

These things I have spoken unto you,
that in me ye might have peace.
In the world ye shall have tribulation:
but be of good cheer;
I have overcome the world.
JOHN 16:33

Jesus gives peace in the midst of trials. Live for Him and He will take care of you.

Jesus answered,
My kingdom is not of this world:
if my kingdom were of this world,
then would my servants fight,
that I should not be delivered to the Jews:
but now is my kingdom not from hence.
JOHN 18:36

Jesus' kingdom is made up of the heart and of the eternal. When you have Him, you have all that you need.

When Jesus therefore had received the vinegar,
he said, It is finished:
and he bowed his head,
and gave up the ghost.
JOHN 19:30

This is not a cry of defeat but a shout of victory. God's plan of salvation was accomplished when Jesus died on the cross. Praise the Lord! It is finished!

But these are written,
that ye might believe that
Jesus is the Christ,
the Son of God;
and that believing ye might have
life through his name.
JOHN 20:31

Jesus Christ is God's Son who came to save us from our sins. Do you know Him personally?

So when they had dined,
Jesus saith to Simon Peter,
Simon, son of Jonas,
lovest thou me more than these?
He saith unto him, Yea, Lord;
thou knowest that I love thee.
He saith unto him, Feed my lambs.
JOHN 21:15

Jesus wants our love most of all. If He has that, He has all of us. Let's love Him with everything we have.

Acts

But ye shall receive power,
after that the Holy Ghost
is come upon you:
and ye shall be witnesses unto me
both in Jerusalem,
and in all Judaea,
and in Samaria,
and unto the uttermost part
of the earth.
ACTS 1:8

The Holy Spirit will empower us to live and share our faith. Let others see Jesus in you. This verse is also the ultimate call to missions. We are not finished until the whole world knows about Jesus.

And it shall come to pass in the last days,
saith God, I will pour out of my Spirit
upon all flesh:
and your sons and
your daughters shall prophesy,
and your young men shall see visions,
and your old men shall dream dreams.
ACTS 2:17

When the Spirit of God moves, great things happen. May God pour His Spirit on His people in wonderful ways today.

Then Peter said,
Silver and gold have I none;
but such as I have give I thee:
In the name of Jesus Christ of Nazareth
rise up and walk.
ACTS 3:6

Jesus will give you much more than what money can buy. When you believe in Him, He will bless your life beyond any expectations. Christians, let's not forget that it isn't money and programs that will make the difference. Jessu is our message.

And Joses,
who by the apostles was surnamed Barnabas,
(which is, being interpreted,
The son of consolation,) a Levite,
and of the country of Cyprus. . .
ACTS 4:36

"Son of consolation" means encourager. May God raise up more encouragers among us.

―――――

Then the twelve called the multitude
of the disciples unto them, and said,
It is not reason that we should leave
the word of God, and serve tables.
Wherefore, brethren,
look ye out among you
seven men of honest report,
full of the Holy Ghost and wisdom,
whom we may appoint over this business.
But we will give ourselves continually to prayer,
and to the ministry of the word.
ACTS 6:2–4

It's important that spiritual leaders take time to study the Bible and pray. God's people are depending on these shepherds.

And when Simon saw that
through laying on of the apostles' hands
the Holy Ghost was given,
he offered them money, Saying,
Give me also this power,
that on whomsoever I lay hands,
he may receive the Holy Ghost.
But Peter said unto him,
Thy money perish with thee,
because thou hast thought that
the gift of God may be purchased with money.
ACTS 8:18–20

You can't buy favors from God. What He wants from us is our love and obedience.

———◇◇◇———

Now there was at Joppa
a certain disciple named Tabitha,
which by interpretation is called Dorcas:
this woman was full of good works
and almsdeeds which she did.
ACTS 9:36

This world needs more people like Dorcas. Be a real disciple. Allow Christ to live His life through you.

For he was a good man,
and full of the Holy Ghost and of faith:
and much people was added unto the Lord.
ACTS 11:24

We need such good men and women today. Can God count on you?

———

Peter therefore was kept in prison:
but prayer was made without ceasing
of the church unto God for him.
ACTS 12:5

Prayer does make a difference. Pray for someone in need. God is waiting to do great things in your life and in the lives of others.

———

Be it known unto you therefore,
men and brethren,
that through this man is preached
unto you the forgiveness of sins.
ACTS 13:38

There's only one way to be forgiven of your sins. You must confess them to Jesus and ask Him to forgive you.

Sirs, why do ye these things?
We also are men of like passions with you,
and preach unto you that ye should turn
from these vanities unto the living God,
which made heaven, and earth,
and the sea, and all things that are therein.
ACTS 14:15

Worship of self, others, and things fails to bring real satisfaction. We are made to worship the living God who created all things.

—*∾*—

But we believe that through the grace
of the Lord Jesus Christ
we shall be saved, even as they.
ACTS 15:11

We are not saved from sin and hell by our own good deeds. We are saved by the grace and mercy of Jesus Christ. Have you accepted God's gift of salvation? "For by grace are ye saved through faith; and that not of yourselves: it is the gift of God: Not of works, lest any man should boast" (Ephesians 2:8–9).

And [the keeper of the prison] brought them out,
and said,
Sirs, what must I do to be saved?
And they said,
Believe on the Lord Jesus Christ,
and thou shalt be saved,
and thy house.
ACTS 16:30–31

Are you, too, looking for forgiveness for the past, help for the present, and the promise of eternal life in heaven? Faith in Jesus is the only way to have all of the above. Have you given your life to Him?

And when they found them not,
they drew Jason and certain brethren
unto the rulers of the city, crying,
These that have turned the world
upside down are come hither also.
ACTS 17:6

When Christians make a difference in this world, those in power take notice. Turn your world upside down for the glory of God.

Many of them also which used curious arts
brought their books together,
and burned them before all men:
and they counted the price of them,
and found it fifty thousand pieces of silver.
So mightily grew the word of
God and prevailed.
ACTS 19:19–20

When people get right with God, the Word of the Lord has great power. May we have a great revival like this.

—∾—

I have showed you all things,
how that so labouring
ye ought to support the weak,
and to remember the words of the Lord Jesus,
how he said,
It is more blessed to give than to receive.
ACTS 20:35

It's nice to receive, but it's better to give. Let's follow Jesus' example of giving. He gave His best and His all.

And one Ananias,
a devout man according to the law,
having a good report of
all the Jews which dwelt there,
Came unto me, and stood,
and said unto me, Brother Saul,
receive thy sight.
And the same hour I looked up upon him.
ACTS 22:12–13

We need more men like Ananias. Do you have a good testimony before others? It makes a difference.

And Paul, earnestly beholding the council,
said, Men and brethren,
I have lived in all good conscience
before God until this day.
ACTS 23:1

There's only one way to have this kind of peace. A person must surrender himself to the Lord.

And herein do I exercise myself,
to have always a conscience void of
offence toward God,
and toward men.
ACTS 24:16

Stop thinking about self and think about the Lord. Also, think about others and their needs. This is the path to peace.

———∽∽∽———

But showed first
unto them of Damascus,
and at Jerusalem,
and throughout all
the coasts of Judaea,
and then to the Gentiles,
that they should repent
and turn to God,
and do works meet for repentance.
ACTS 26:20

The Christian life is one that has repented of sin. Jesus came to save us from our sins, not in our sins. Repent and turn your life over to God.

Romans

For there is no respect of persons with God.
ROMANS 2:11

The ground is level at the foot of the cross. God does not play favorites. He wants everyone to come to the Christian faith.

———※———

As it is written,
There is none righteous,
no, not one.
ROMANS 3:10

All of us need God's grace and forgiveness. "For all have sinned, and come short of the glory of God" (Romans 3:23).

For what saith the scripture?
Abraham believed God,
and it was counted unto him for righteousness.
ROMANS 4:3

Salvation does not come because of our good works. It comes by faith in Jesus and what He did for us on the cross. Are you saved?

―⦚―

But God commendeth his love toward us,
in that, while we were yet sinners,
Christ died for us.
ROMANS 5:8

Don't ever doubt God loves you. Remember the cross and know that He does.

―⦚―

And we know that all things work together
for good to them that love God,
to them who are the called
according to his purpose.
ROMANS 8:28

This promise is made to those who love God. Does this include you?

So then faith cometh by hearing,
and hearing by the word of God.
ROMANS 10:17

Do you really want to increase your faith in God? Read the Bible, and then apply God's Word to your life.

—◆—

And be not conformed to this world:
but be ye transformed by
the renewing of your mind,
that ye may prove what is that good,
and acceptable, and perfect, will of God.
ROMANS 12:2

Real Christians are changed people. "Therefore if any man be in Christ, he is a new creature: old things are passed away; behold, all things are become new" (2 Corinthians 5:17).

—◆—

Owe no man any thing, but to love one another:
for he that loveth another hath fulfilled the law.
ROMANS 13:8

Here's a recipe for good living: Pay your debts. Love the Lord and your family, friends, and coworkers.

So then every one of us shall give
account of himself to God.
ROMANS 14:12

You can't get around this. God made us and we are accountable to Him. Are you ready to meet God? You are if you have Jesus as your Lord and Savior.

Now the God of patience and
consolation grant you to be likeminded
one toward another
according to Christ Jesus:
That ye may with one mind
and one mouth glorify God,
even the Father of our Lord Jesus Christ.
Wherefore receive ye one another,
as Christ also received us to the glory of God.
ROMANS 15:5–7

May a spirit of unity built upon the Bible arise among God's people today. Let's love and encourage one another. This will be a great testimony to the world.

1 Corinthians

*For the preaching of the cross is
to them that perish foolishness;
but unto us which are saved
it is the power of God.*
1 CORINTHIANS 1:18

I love the preaching of the cross of Jesus because
I know that Jesus paid the price for my sins there.
Thank You, Jesus.

---

*Because the foolishness of God is wiser than men;
and the weakness of God is stronger than men.*
1 CORINTHIANS 1:25

We can sometimes think that we are so smart.
Compared to God, we know nothing. This is why
we need to put our faith in Him.

But as it is written,
Eye hath not seen, nor ear heard,
neither have entered into the heart of man,
the things which God hath prepared
for them that love him.
1 CORINTHIANS 2:9

We serve a great and loving God who has promised to take care of us. "Call unto me, and I will answer thee, and show thee great and mighty things, which thou knowest not" (Jeremiah 33:3).

———

For other foundation can no man lay
than that is laid, which is Jesus Christ.
1 CORINTHIANS 3:11

Jesus is the only foundation that will stand the storms of life and eternity. Put your trust in Him.

———

Wherefore I beseech you,
be ye followers of me.
1 CORINTHIANS 4:16

Christians, could you make such a bold statement to others? Is your life one that others could imitate?

Your glorying is not good.
Know ye not that a little leaven
leaveneth the whole lump?
1 CORINTHIANS 5:6

Don't give sin a toe-hold in your life. One day such action will have severe consequences.

———∞———

Flee fornication.
Every sin that a man doeth is without the body;
but he that committeth fornication
sinneth against his own body.
1 CORINTHIANS 6:18

Sexual immorality carries a high price. Live life God's moral way and experience His blessings.

———∞———

And unto the married I command,
yet not I, but the Lord,
Let not the wife depart from her husband.
1 CORINTHIANS 7:10

A marriage and a family are worth saving. Give all marital problems to God and let Him renew love in your heart for your spouse.

But take heed lest by any means
this liberty of yours become a
stumblingblock to them that are weak.
1 CORINTHIANS 8:9

Yes, we are free in Christ. However, we must be sensitive to what our lives say to others. Don't be a stumbling block to someone else. Live a holy life.

And every man that
striveth for the mastery
is temperate in all things.
Now they do it to obtain
a corruptible crown;
but we an incorruptible.
1 CORINTHIANS 9:25

There are great rewards in serving Jesus, rewards that will never rust or rot. Don't forget that Jesus has prepared heaven and all its splendor for us to enjoy. "Let not your heart be troubled: ye believe in God, believe also in me. In my Father's house are many mansions: if it were not so, I would have told you. I go to prepare a place for you" (John 14:1–2). "Serve the Lord with gladness."

There hath no temptation taken you
but such as is common to man:
but God is faithful,
who will not suffer you to be
tempted above that ye are able;
but will with the temptation also
make a way to escape,
that ye may be able to bear it.
1 CORINTHIANS 10:13

You are not alone when you face temptation. Jesus will give you the strength to overcome any temptation. By the way, one way of escape is Psalm 119:11, which says: "Thy word have I hid in mine heart, that I might not sin against thee." Trust Him now.

———

And now abideth
faith, hope, charity, these three;
but the greatest of these is charity.
1 CORINTHIANS 13:13

There's nothing like the love of God. Let His love flood your life.

For as in Adam all die,
even so in Christ shall all be made alive.
1 CORINTHIANS 15:22

In Christ we have the victory over death since He has already conquered death for us. Are you in Christ?

———

Let all your things be done with charity.
1 CORINTHIANS 16:14

Whatever you say or do, make certain that it is seasoned with love. This is one of the best testimonies that a Christian can give.

2 Corinthians

Who comforteth us in all our tribulation,
that we may be able to comfort them
which are in any trouble,
by the comfort wherewith we ourselves
are comforted of God.
2 CORINTHIANS 1:4

The blessings of God's comfort should never stop with us. Let's help others who are hurting.

———

Now thanks be unto God,
which always causeth us to triumph in Christ,
and maketh manifest the savour of
his knowledge by us in every place.
2 CORINTHIANS 2:14

There's a wonderful victory in Jesus. Trust Him in every situation.

Now the Lord is that Spirit:
and where the Spirit of the Lord is,
there is liberty.
2 CORINTHIANS 3:17

Real freedom is ours when we allow the Spirit of the Lord to rule our lives.

———

For we preach not ourselves,
but Christ Jesus the Lord;
and ourselves your servants for Jesus' sake.
2 CORINTHIANS 4:5

Our lives and conversations should center on the person of Jesus Christ. He is the One who gives hope and meaning to life.

———

Therefore if any man be in Christ,
he is a new creature:
old things are passed away;
behold, all things are become new.
2 CORINTHIANS 5:17

Jesus can give you the new life and attitude that you need. Allow Him to take control of your life.

Be ye not unequally yoked together
with unbelievers:
for what fellowship hath
righteousness with unrighteousness?
and what communion hath
light with darkness?
2 CORINTHIANS 6:14

Christians, let's make sure that our commitments and relationships are in good standing with the Lord. He knows what is best for us.

—∿—

Having therefore these promises,
dearly beloved,
let us cleanse ourselves from all filthiness
of the flesh and spirit,
perfecting holiness in the fear of God.
2 CORINTHIANS 7:1

Sometimes our lives need a good "housecleaning." Let's rid ourselves of unrighteousness and fill our hearts and minds with thoughts of God.

For ye know the grace of
our Lord Jesus Christ, that,
though he was rich,
yet for your sakes he became poor,
that ye through his poverty might be rich.
2 CORINTHIANS 8:9

Jesus gave up the splendor of heaven to die for our sins on earth. Let's not forget what Jesus did for us. "For God so loved the world, that he gave his only begotten Son, that whosoever believeth in him should not perish, but have everlasting life" (John 3:16).

Every man according
as he purposeth in his heart,
so let him give; not grudgingly,
or of necessity:
for God loveth a cheerful giver.
2 CORINTHIANS 9:7

The Lord loves to give and so should His people. When you give, give with a happy, willing heart. This really pleases the Lord.

(For the weapons of our warfare are not carnal,
but mighty through God to
the pulling down of strong holds;)
Casting down imaginations,
and every high thing that exalteth itself
against the knowledge of God,
and bringing into captivity
every thought to the obedience of Christ.
2 CORINTHIANS 10:4–5

As Christians we realize that the forces that move and motivate this world are spiritual. We should gladly acknowledge the Lord's power and His love.

———

For such are false apostles, deceitful workers,
transforming themselves into the apostles of Christ.
And no marvel;
for Satan himself is transformed
into an angel of light.
2 CORINTHIANS 11:13–14

Don't put faith in everything you read or hear. Check it out. If it doesn't agree with the Bible, there's a problem. Don't be deceived by half-truths.

And he said unto me,
My grace is sufficient for thee:
for my strength is made perfect in weakness.
Most gladly therefore will I
rather glory in my infirmities,
that the power of Christ may rest upon me.
2 CORINTHIANS 12:9

The Lord has the power you need. Cast your cares upon Him. Our weaknesses can be a doorway to receiving God's special grace to meet our needs.

Examine yourselves,
whether ye be in the faith;
prove your own selves.
Know ye not your own selves,
how that Jesus Christ is in you,
except ye be reprobates?
2 CORINTHIANS 13:5

Are you really saved or just a religious person? You can know about God but not know Him personally. "Not every one that saith unto me, 'Lord, Lord,' shall enter into the kingdom of heaven; but he that doeth the will of my Father which is in heaven" (Matthew 7:21).

Galatians

Knowing that a man is not justified
by the works of the law,
but by the faith of Jesus Christ,
even we have believed in Jesus Christ,
that we might be justified by the faith of Christ,
and not by the works of the law.
GALATIANS 2:16

No one is good enough to work his way to heaven.

I am crucified with Christ: nevertheless I live;
yet not I, but Christ liveth in me.
GALATIANS 2:20

The Christian life is one surrendered to Jesus.
People should see Jesus in us.

But the fruit of the Spirit is
love, joy, peace, longsuffering,
gentleness, goodness, faith,
Meekness, temperance:
against such there is no law.
GALATIANS 5:22–23

The Lord produces wonderful virtues in His people when we let Him truly be the Lord of our lives. Let go and let God have His wonderful way in your life.

—⚬⚬⚬—

But God forbid that I should glory,
save in the cross of our Lord Jesus Christ,
by whom the world is crucified unto me,
and I unto the world.
GALATIANS 6:14

Thank God for the cross. It was there that Jesus paid our sin debt.

Ephesians

In whom we have redemption through his blood,
the forgiveness of sins,
according to the riches of his grace.
EPHESIANS 1:7

"What can wash away my sin? Nothing but the blood of Jesus. What can make me whole again? Nothing but the blood of Jesus."

———— ⌇⌇⌇ ————

For by grace are ye saved through faith;
and that not of yourselves:
it is the gift of God:
Not of works, lest any man should boast.
EPHESIANS 2:8–9

We don't work or earn our way to heaven. Salvation is a gift from God. Accept His gift for your life.

*Now unto him that is able to do exceeding
abundantly above all that we ask or think,
according to the power that worketh in us,
Unto him be glory in the church by
Christ Jesus throughout all ages,
world without end. Amen.*
EPHESIANS 3:20–21

Put your trust in God. He is able to do more than you could ever dream.

—∞—

*But speaking the truth in love,
may grow up into him in all things,
which is the head, even Christ.*
EPHESIANS 4:15

Jesus spoke the truth in love and so should we. God's love is the strongest force on earth.

—∞—

*And be ye kind one to another,
tenderhearted, forgiving one another,
even as God for Christ's sake hath forgiven you.*
EPHESIANS 4:32

The world needs this kind of Christianity. Be a real Christian.

*Nevertheless let every one of you
in particular so love his wife even as himself;
and the wife see that she reverence her husband.*
EPHESIANS 5:33

Many failed marriages could have survived if this one verse were followed. Husbands, love your wives. Wives, love your husbands with respect.

———

*Children,
obey your parents in the Lord:
for this is right.
Honour thy father and mother;
which is the
first commandment with promise;
that it may be well with thee,
and thou mayest live long on the earth.*
EPHESIANS 6:1–3

Children will do these things only if they are taught. Parents, take time to teach your children. The foundation for family and society is found in the Bible. Remember, all of these are God's ideas. Therefore, He knows what is best.

Finally, my brethren,
be strong in the Lord,
and in the power of his might.
Put on the whole armour of God,
that ye may be able to stand against
the wiles of the devil.
EPHESIANS 6:10–11

There is a spiritual war taking place in our land. To be prepared, God's people must clothe themselves in His armor. In other words, read the Bible and pray.

Philippians

For to me to live is Christ, and to die is gain.
PHILIPPIANS 1:21

This should be the motto of every believer in Jesus.

———

For it is God which worketh in you
both to will and to do of his good pleasure.
PHILIPPIANS 2:13

Let go and let God have His way in your life. He can make your life something wonderful.

———

Rejoice in the Lord alway:
and again I say, Rejoice.
PHILIPPIANS 4:4

Let your joy come from Jesus, who never changes.

Be careful for nothing;
but in every thing by prayer
and supplication with thanksgiving
let your requests be made known unto God.
And the peace of God,
which passeth all understanding,
shall keep your hearts
and minds through Christ Jesus.
PHILIPPIANS 4:6–7

Tell the Lord where it hurts and He will give you the peace you need.

—∞—

I can do all things through
Christ which strengtheneth me.
PHILIPPIANS 4:13

There's no telling what God can do in and through you. Let Him be your strength.

—∞—

But my God shall supply all your need
according to his riches in glory by Christ Jesus.
PHILIPPIANS 4:19

Worry does nothing but drain energy from us. Don't worry. Put your trust in the Lord.

Colossians

As ye have therefore received
Christ Jesus the Lord,
so walk ye in him.
COLOSSIANS 2:6

Jesus is not just for the future. We are to walk with Him daily. Fellowship with Him brings love, joy, and peace.

———

Let the word of Christ dwell
in you richly in all wisdom;
teaching and admonishing one another
in psalms and hymns and spiritual songs,
singing with grace in your hearts to the Lord.
COLOSSIANS 3:16

Are you down? Read the Word and let your voice sing to the Lord. You will see a difference!

Continue in prayer,
and watch in the same with thanksgiving.
COLOSSIANS 4:2

Prayer should ever be a part of our daily lives. Take time to pray.

1 Thessalonians

For our gospel came not unto you in word only,
but also in power, and in the Holy Ghost,
and in much assurance; as ye know what
manner of men we were among you for your sake.
1 THESSALONIANS 1:5

Does "our gospel" mean doing more than saying words? Let's live a life pleasing to God.

But as we were allowed of God
to be put in trust with the gospel,
even so we speak;
not as pleasing men, but God,
which trieth our hearts.
1 THESSALONIANS 2:4

Are you trying to please men or God? The Lord's will should be our priority.

For the Lord himself shall descend
from heaven with a shout,
with the voice of the archangel,
and with the trump of God:
and the dead in Christ shall rise first.
1 THESSALONIANS 4:16

Jesus is coming back. Are you ready?

Rejoice evermore.
Pray without ceasing.
In every thing give thanks:
for this is the will of God
in Christ Jesus concerning you.
1 THESSALONIANS 5:16–18

Here's good advice for all who long to live the great life.

2 Thessalonians

Wherefore also we pray always for you,
that our God would count you
worthy of this calling,
and fulfil all the good pleasure of his goodness,
and the work of faith with power.
2 THESSALONIANS 1:11

Christians, are we living up to the calling of our Lord? As believers, remember that we bear His name.

—~~—

Even him, whose coming is
after the working of Satan with
all power and signs and lying wonders. . .
2 THESSALONIANS 2:9

The devil has his bag of tricks. Don't be deceived. This is why it is so important that we know and love God's Word, the Bible.

And for this cause God shall
send them strong delusion,
that they should believe a lie:
That they all might be damned
who believed not the truth,
but had pleasure in unrighteousness.
2 THESSALONIANS 2:11–12

The consequences of sin and unbelief are horrible. People so want to believe the lies of Satan that God gives them up to their own deceits. Pray that societies will be awakened out of their spiritual slumber.

But ye, brethren,
be not weary in well doing.
2 THESSALONIANS 3:13

Dear Christians, stay faithful. God will make a difference through us.

1 Timothy

This is a faithful saying,
and worthy of all acceptation,
that Christ Jesus came into the world to save sinners;
of whom I am chief.
1 TIMOTHY 1:15

All of God's people are nothing without the grace and salvation of God in Jesus Christ. Thank God He saved us from sins and hell.

———

For there is one God,
and one mediator between God and men,
the man Christ Jesus.
1 TIMOTHY 2:5

If you want access to God, you must go through Jesus. "Jesus saith unto him, I am the way, the truth, and the life: no man cometh unto the Father, but by me" (John 14:6).

Take heed unto thyself,
and unto the doctrine;
continue in them:
for in doing this
thou shalt both save thyself,
and them that hear thee.
1 TIMOTHY 4:16

Doctrine is that upon which we base our beliefs and behavior. Make sure that your life is based on the doctrine of Christianity, that is, on Jesus and the teachings of His Word.

—⚬—

Let the elders that rule well
be counted worthy of double honour,
especially they who labour in
the word and doctrine.
1 TIMOTHY 5:17

Respect and pray for those who preach and teach the Word of God. They have an awesome responsibility.

2 Timothy

Study to show thyself approved unto God,
a workman that needeth not to be ashamed,
rightly dividing the word of truth.
But shun profane and vain babblings:
for they will increase unto more ungodliness.
2 TIMOTHY 2:15–16

Spiritual growth is no accident. To grow as Christians we must study God's Word and avoid idle chatter.

I have fought a good fight,
I have finished my course,
I have kept the faith.
2 TIMOTHY 4:7

May this be our testimony. Let's finish strong for the glory of God.

Titus

In hope of eternal life, which God,
that cannot lie,
promised before the world began. . .
TITUS 1:2

Here's something that God cannot do. He cannot lie. God always keeps His Word and His promises.

———◆———

They profess that they know God;
but in works they deny him,
being abominable, and disobedient,
and unto every good work reprobate.
TITUS 1:16

Being a child of God is more than just professing faith in Jesus. Living a Christian life means being a changed person.

For the grace of God that bringeth salvation
hath appeared to all men,
Teaching us that,
denying ungodliness and worldly lusts,
we should live soberly,
righteously, and godly,
in this present world.
TITUS 2:11–12

When people are born again they become godly people. Can others see Jesus in you?

⟿

Not by works of righteousness
which we have done,
but according to his mercy he saved us,
by the washing of regeneration,
and renewing of the Holy Ghost.
TITUS 3:5

We are saved from hell by God's grace and mercy alone. Cast your life on the mercy of God before it's too late.

Philemon

I thank my God,
making mention of thee
always in my prayers.
PHILEMON 4

A praying friend is the best friend. Be a best friend.

———

I beseech thee for my son Onesimus,
whom I have begotten in my bonds.
PHILEMON 10

Before Onesimus became a Christian, he was not so much good. However, after he came to Jesus, he became a blessing. That's what Jesus can do for anyone.

Hebrews

God, who at sundry times and in divers manners
spake in time past unto the fathers by the prophets,
Hath in these last days spoken unto us by his Son,
whom he hath appointed heir of all things,
by whom also he made the worlds.
HEBREWS 1:1–2

The ultimate expression of God's love for us is
when God the Son became the man Christ Jesus.

―∾―

How shall we escape, if we neglect so great salvation;
which at the first began to be spoken by the Lord,
and was confirmed unto us by them that heard him.
HEBREWS 2:3

It is inexcusable to refuse God's salvation in Jesus
Christ. Crown Jesus Lord of your life before it is
everlastingly too late.

But exhort one another daily,
while it is called To day;
lest any of you be hardened
through the deceitfulness of sin.
HEBREWS 3:13

We need to help each other recognize the deceitfulness of sin. If we don't, our hearts will become hardened against God. This encouragement is not to be occasional, but rather consistent and daily.

―――∾∾―――

For the word of God is quick, and powerful,
and sharper than any twoedged sword,
piercing even to the dividing asunder
of soul and spirit,
and of the joints and marrow,
and is a discerner of the thoughts
and intents of the heart.
HEBREWS 4:12

The Bible speaks to the heart as no other book. Let God speak to you through His Word.

Wherefore he is able also to
save them to the uttermost
that come unto God by him,
seeing he ever liveth
to make intercession for them.
HEBREWS 7:25

You're not too far gone for God to help you. He can and will save you from the penalty of sin, if you give your life to Him.

―∞―

Not forsaking the assembling
of ourselves together,
as the manner of some is;
but exhorting one another:
and so much the more,
as ye see the day approaching.
HEBREWS 10:25

Worship attendance is important. It's amazing the silly excuses people give for neglecting worship of God. Quit giving excuses. Go to church to receive and to give Christian encouragement.

But without faith it is impossible
to please him:
for he that cometh to God
must believe that he is,
and that he is a rewarder of
them that diligently seek him.
HEBREWS 11:6

You and I cannot please God without faith. That said, how can you increase your faith? "So then faith cometh by hearing, and hearing by the word of God" (Romans 10:17).

———⟨∾⟩———

Wherefore we receiving a kingdom
which cannot be moved,
let us have grace,
whereby we may serve God acceptably
with reverence and godly fear:
For our God is a consuming fire.
HEBREWS 12:28–29

Our Lord is not only to be loved but He is also to be feared. Give Him the respect He deserves.

Jesus Christ the same yesterday,
and to day,
and for ever.
HEBREWS 13:8

You can always count on Jesus. He never changes.

James

Every good gift and
every perfect gift is from above,
and cometh down from the Father of lights,
with whom is no variableness,
neither shadow of turning.
JAMES 1:17

Hell is a terrible place. Because all good gifts come from God, there won't be one ounce of goodness in hell. Give your life to Jesus before it's too late.

Wherefore, my beloved brethren,
let every man be swift to hear,
slow to speak, slow to wrath.
JAMES 1:19

We would save ourselves a lot of grief if we would follow this instruction. God will help us.

Thou believest that there is one God;
thou doest well: the devils also believe,
and tremble.
JAMES 2:19

It has been said that many people miss heaven by eighteen inches. That's the distance from the head to the heart. Salvation comes by a heart commitment to Jesus, not by mere head knowledge.

———

Out of the same mouth proceedeth
blessing and cursing.
My brethren,
these things ought not so to be.
JAMES 3:10

Are you sending mixed signals? Let your conversations honor the Lord.

———

Humble yourselves in the sight of the Lord,
and he shall lift you up.
JAMES 4:10

Humility must come before God can bestow honor. Humility is a door to true greatness.

Confess your faults one to another,
and pray one for another,
that ye may be healed.
The effectual fervent prayer of
a righteous man availeth much.
JAMES 5:16

The prayer of a righteous man has tremendous power and influence. Take time to pray. It works.

1 Peter

For all flesh is as grass,
and all the glory of man
as the flower of grass.
The grass withereth,
and the flower thereof falleth away:
But the word of the Lord endureth for ever.
And this is the word which by
the gospel is preached unto you.
1 PETER 1:24–25

People come and go but God's Word stands forever. You can trust God's Word. It is powerful and influential. "For the word of God is quick, and powerful, and sharper than any twoedged sword, piercing even to the dividing asunder of soul and spirit, and of the joints and marrow, and is a discerner of the thoughts and intents of the heart" (Hebrews 4:12).

But ye are a chosen generation,
a royal priesthood, an holy nation,
a peculiar people;
that ye should show forth
the praises of him who hath
called you out of darkness
into his marvellous light.
1 PETER 2:9

Every Christian is somebody. God has a wonderful plan for your life.

Likewise, ye husbands,
dwell with them according to knowledge,
giving honour unto the wife,
as unto the weaker vessel,
and as being heirs together
of the grace of life;
that your prayers be not hindered.
1 PETER 3:7

Our world needs loving, compassionate, praying husbands. Husband, it's hard to pray when things are not right at home. Love your wife and care for her.

For Christ also hath once suffered for sins,
the just for the unjust,
that he might bring us to God,
being put to death in the flesh,
but quickened by the Spirit.
1 PETER 3:18

Jesus paid the price for our sins. We should gladly serve Him.

—⁂—

And above all things have
fervent charity among yourselves:
for charity shall cover the multitude of sins.
1 PETER 4:8

The love of God in our hearts can set many wrong things right. Allow His love to make a difference in you.

—⁂—

Casting all your care upon him;
for he careth for you.
1 PETER 5:7

Jesus loves you. You don't have to carry that load. Cast your cares upon Him.

2 Peter

For the prophecy came not in old time
by the will of man:
but holy men of God spake
as they were moved by the Holy Ghost.
2 PETER 1:21

The Bible is the inspired Word of God. You can
always depend on His Word.

But grow in grace,
and in the knowledge of our
Lord and Saviour Jesus Christ.
To him be glory both now and for ever. Amen.
2 PETER 3:18

Spiritual growth should be the goal of every
Christian. How are you doing?

1 John

If we confess our sins,
he is faithful and just to forgive us our sins,
and to cleanse us from all unrighteousness.
1 JOHN 1:9

You can't get on with your life until you get right
with God. Confess your sins to God and let Him
cleanse you.

———

And the world passeth away,
and the lust thereof:
but he that doeth the
will of God abideth for ever.
1 JOHN 2:17

When men and women who love the Lord do His
will, their actions have eternal value.

My little children, let us not love in word,
neither in tongue; but in deed and in truth.
1 JOHN 3:18

Love is more than just words. Love shows itself in actions of kindness and unselfishness.

———

Ye are of God, little children,
and have overcome them:
because greater is he that is in you,
than he that is in the world.
1 JOHN 4:4

The power of God within you is greater than the problems or sin you face. Let go and let God give you the victory.

———

And this is the record,
that God hath given to us eternal life,
and this life is in his Son.
He that hath the Son hath life;
and he that hath not the Son of God hath not life.
1 JOHN 5:11–12

If you have Jesus, you have life. If you don't have Him, you don't. Where do you stand?

These things have I written
unto you that believe on
the name of the Son of God;
that ye may know that ye have eternal life,
and that ye may believe on the name of
the Son of God.
1 JOHN 5:13

One of the reasons God gave us the Bible was that we could have a written guarantee that He keeps His Word. God wants you to know that you belong to Him.

2 John

I rejoiced greatly that I found
of thy children walking in truth,
as we have received
a commandment from the Father.
2 JOHN 4

One of the greatest blessings of life is to see our children walk in the truth of God. One of the greatest heartaches is to see them destroy their lives. On which path are we leading them?

———

And this is love,
that we walk after his commandments.
2 JOHN 6

It can't be any simpler than this. This is the life of a true disciple of Jesus. "If ye love me, keep my commandments" (John 14:15).

3 John

Beloved, I wish above all things that
thou mayest prosper and be in health,
even as thy soul prospereth.
3 JOHN 2

The Lord wants the best for you. Follow Him
and things will be well with you.

———✦———

Beloved, follow not that which is evil,
but that which is good.
He that doeth good is of God:
but he that doeth evil hath not seen God.
3 JOHN 11

A Christian life is a life filled with goodness and
good deeds. Can others see Jesus in us?

Jude

*It was needful for me to write unto you,
and exhort you that ye should earnestly
contend for the faith which
was once delivered unto the saints.*
JUDE 3

We can't be lazy concerning our faith in Jesus. We must be diligent and consistent in knowing and sharing the Gospel.

———

*Even as Sodom and Gomorrha. . .
are set forth for an example,
suffering the vengeance of eternal fire.*
JUDE 7

Will we ever learn from history? Look at Sodom and Gomorrah. Sin has terrible consequences.

Revelation

I am Alpha and Omega,
the beginning and the ending,
saith the Lord, which is,
and which was,
and which is to come, the Almighty.
REVELATION 1:8

God began this world and He will end it. To assure our eternal future, it's wise to put our lives into His hands.

Nevertheless I have somewhat against thee,
because thou hast left thy first love.
REVELATION 2:4

Christians, have you stopped loving the Lord as you should? Remember what He did for you on the cross.

Behold,
I stand at the door, and knock:
if any man hear my voice,
and open the door,
I will come in to him,
and will sup with him,
and he with me.
REVELATION 3:20

Jesus is waiting for you to open the door to Him. Do it today. It's a privilege to have the Son of God love you, die for you, be resurrected for you, and now speak to your heart.

Thou art worthy, O Lord,
to receive glory and honour and power:
for thou hast created all things,
and for thy pleasure
they are and were created.
REVELATION 4:11

We must remember that this world is on loan to us. It belongs to God. Let's honor Him by our obedience and worship.

For the Lamb
which is in the midst of
the throne shall feed them,
and shall lead them unto
living fountains of waters:
and God shall wipe away
all tears from their eyes.
REVELATION 7:17

Trust the Lord. He can and will wipe away the tears from your life. He loves you.

———✥———

And the rest of the men which were not
killed by these plagues yet repented
not of the works of their hands,
that they should not worship devils,
and idols of gold, and silver, and brass,
and stone, and of wood:
which neither can see, nor hear, nor walk:
Neither repented they of their murders,
nor of their sorceries, nor of their fornication,
nor of their thefts.
REVELATION 9:20–21

Hardening your heart toward God spells certain doom. Repent of your sin before it is everlastingly too late.

And men were scorched with great heat,
and blasphemed the name of God,
which hath power over these plagues:
and they repented not to give him glory.
REVELATION 16:9

God uses judgment to get our attention. It's up to us to repent of our sins and draw close to Him.

And whosoever was not found
written in the book of life
was cast into the lake of fire.
REVELATION 20:15

Have you given your life to Jesus? It's important. Having faith in Jesus is the only way to get your name in the book of life. "Jesus saith unto him, I am the way, the truth, and the life: no man cometh unto the Father, but by me" (John 14:6). If you don't, you will spend eternity in hell. The decision is yours to make. Give your life to Jesus today before it's too late.

And God shall wipe away
all tears from their eyes;
and there shall be no more death,
neither sorrow, nor crying,
neither shall there be any more pain:
for the former things are passed away.
REVELATION 21:4

Heaven is a wonderful place prepared for God's people. And Jesus is the only way to get there.

Topical Index

9:25, 16:14; 2 Corinthians 7:1, 13:5;
Galatians 2:20; Philippians 1:21;
Colossians 2:6; 2 Thessalonians 3:13;
1 Timothy 4:16; Titus 2:11–12;
Philemon 10; 1 Peter 2:9; 2 Peter 3:18;
2 John 4, 6; 3 John 11

Encouragement—Exodus 17:12; 1 Samuel 23:16,
30:6; Acts 4:36

Eternal Life—2 Samuel 12:23; Job 14:14;

Faith—Genesis 15:6; Psalm 20:7;
Matthew 14–30; Mark 2:3, 5:36, 9:23–24;
Romans 4:3, 10:17; Hebrews 11:6;
James 2:19; 1 John 5:13

Forgiveness—Psalm 103:12, 130:3–4;
Mark 11:25; Luke 17:4–5, 23:34;
Acts 13:38; 1 John 1:9

Freedom—John 8:36; 2 Corinthians 3:17

Friends—Proverbs 13:20, 17:17, 25:19, 27:17

Giving—Exodus 35:21; Leviticus 23:22, 27:30;
Numbers 18:29; Deuteronomy 16:17;
2 Samuel 24:24; Ezra 2:68; Proverbs 3:9–10;

Malachi 3:10; Luke 21:3–4; Acts 20:35;
2 Corinthians 9:7

God's
> Blessings—Numbers 25:10–12; 1 Chronicles
> 13:14, 2 Chronicles 31:21; Job 42:10
>
> Discipline—Genesis 6:3; Numbers 14:44–45;
> Deuteronomy 8:5; Job 5:17;
> Proverbs 3:11–12
>
> Faithfulness—Genesis 33:5; Exodus 2:25,
> 6:6; Leviticus 11:45; Numbers 23:19;
> Deuteronomy 8:3, 31:8; Joshua 1:1–2,
> 1:5, 1:9, 23:14; Ruth 4:22; 1 Samuel
> 17:37; 2 Samuel 7:22, 22:28; 1 Kings
> 8:56, 19:18; Ezra 1:1; Nehemiah 9:33;
> Psalm 16:8; Lamentations 3:22–23;
> Titus 1:2
>
> Goodness—Genesis 50:20; Numbers 10:32;
> Psalm 84:11; Nahum 1:7; James 1:17
>
> Greatness—Exodus 5:2, 15:18; Deuteronomy
> 4:39; Joshua 6:20; Judges 7:2, 8:23;
> 1 Samuel 2:6–7, 14:6, 17:47; 2 Kings
> 3:18, 6:16; 1 Chronicles 14:15; Ezra 1:2,
> 3:11; Job 1:21, 19:25–26; Psalm 11:4,
> 94:9, 147:4–5; Jeremiah 9:23–24;
> Micah 1:2; Habakkuk 2:20; Haggai 2:8;
> Revelation 1:8

Judgment—Ezekiel 7:9; Obadiah 15

Mercy—Genesis 19:16; Psalm 145:8;

Joel 2:25; Micah 7:18; Nahum 1:3

Power—Exodus 3:14, 4:10–11; Leviticus
19:32; 2 Chronicles 16:9, 20:15, 32:8;
Nehemiah 4:14, 9:6; Psalm 127:1;
Ecclesiastes 3:14; Isaiah 14:27, 40:31,
41:10, 55:9; Jeremiah 32:17, 32:27;
Zechariah 4:6; Matthew 8:26–27;
Luke 1:37, 6:19; John 5:17;
Acts 2:17, 3:6; 1 Corinthians 2:9;
Ephesians 3:20–21

Protection—Exodus 13:21, 14:14, 15:26;
Deuteronomy 1:29–30, 3:22, 31:6;
Psalm 34:7, 34:17, 46:1, 91:2, 118:6;
Song of Solomon 2:4; Daniel 3:25

Provision—Genesis 22:14, 45:7;
Deuteronomy 30:9, 33:25; Psalm 1:3,
34:10, 37:25, 55:22, 60:11, 68:5,
68:19, 145:16, 147:3; Jonah 1:17;
Zephaniah 3:17

Word—Numbers 9:8; Psalm 107:20, 119:89;
Deuteronomy 6:7, 119:105; Isaiah 40:8;
Amos 8:11; Matthew 4:4, 24:35;
Colossians 3:16; Hebrews 4:12;
1 Peter 1:24–25; 2 Peter 1:21

Healing—Acts 22:12–13

Heaven—Matthew 13:33; John 18:36;
    Revelation 7:17, 21:4

Hope—Psalm 39:7

Humility (Pride)—Genesis 11:4; Numbers 12:3;
    2 Chronicles 26:16; Job 14:1; Proverbs
    16:18, 27:1; Isaiah 2:17; Obadiah 3;
    Luke 14:11

Influence—Genesis 13:12–13, 26:18;
    Exodus 23:2, 34:12; Joshua 22:20;
    2 Chronicles 28:19; Ezra 4:4;
    Nehemiah 2:19; Matthew 18:6; Luke 23:24;
    1 Corinthians 5:6; Galatians 5:22–23;
    Hebrews 3:13, 10:25

Integrity—Genesis 4:9; 1 Chronicles 10:4;
    Proverbs 10:9; 1 Timothy 5:17

Jesus
    Crucified—Mark 15:15; John 12:32, 19:30;
        Galatians 6:14
    Lord—Matthew 2:2; Mark 7:37, 12:26–27;
        John 1:1, 14; Hebrews 1:1–2
    Prophecy—Genesis 49:10; Isaiah 7:14, 9:6,
        53:4–6; Micah 5:2

Resurrection—Matthew 28:6; Luke 7:14–15,
20:38, 24:6; John 6:35, 11:25;
1 Corinthians 15:22
Savior—Matthew 1:21, 16:15–16, 17:5,
27:54; 1 Corinthians 3:11; 2 Corinthians
4:5; Galatians 6:14; 1 Timothy 2:5;
Hebrews 13:8
Second Coming—Matthew 25:13;
1 Thessalonians 4:16

Joy—Nehemiah 8:10, 12:43; Psalm 118:24; Luke
10:20; John 7:38, 10:10; Philippians 4:4

Judgment—Genesis 19:14; Numbers 32:23,
33:55; 1 Samuel 3:13, 13:14, 16:7;
2 Samuel 12:12; 2 Kings 20:1; Psalm
7:14–15, 9:17; Proverbs 14:12, 26:27, 29:1;
Isaiah 5:20; Hosea 4:6, 8:7; Amos 4:12;
Zephaniah 1:18; Romans 14:12;
2 Thessalonians 2:11–12; Hebrews 2:3,
12:28–29; Jude 7; Revelation 20:15

Kindness—2 Samuel 9:1; 2 Kings 7:9; Ephesians
4:32

Love—Leviticus 19:18; Deuteronomy 6:4–5;
Ruth 1:16; Proverbs 10:12; Song of Solomon

Peace—Psalm 3:5, 4:8; Isaiah 26:3;
    Matthew 11:28–30; Mark 4:39;
    Luke 8:24; 2 Corinthians 1:4;
    Philippians 4:6–7; 1 Peter 5:7

Perseverance—Ecclesiastes 7:8; 9:10

Prayer—Numbers 6:24–26; 1 Samuel 12:23;
    2 Samuel 2:1; 1 Kings 8:39, 22:5;
    2 Kings 19:14, 22:19; 1 Chronicles 4:10;
    Ezra 8:23; Psalm 37:4, 40:1–2, 65:2, 86:6–7,
    116:1–2, 139:23–24; Jeremiah 33:3;
    Daniel 6:10; Matthew 26:41; Mark 1:35;
    Luke 11:9–10, 18:1; Acts 12:5;
    Romans 15:5–7; Colossians 4:2;
    2 Thessalonians 1:11; Philemon 4;
    James 5:16

Purity—Job 31:1; Isaiah 6:3

Repentance—Judges 2:2; 2 Samuel 12:13;
    2 Kings 22:11; 2 Chronicles 30:7, 34:27;
    Isaiah 55:7; Jeremiah 2:5; Ezekiel 14:6,
    18:32; Matthew 9:12–13; Mark 6:12;
    Luke 13:3; Acts 26:20; Revelation 2:4,
    9:20–21, 16:9

Revival—Exodus 24:7; Judg
    1 Samuel 7:3–4; 2 Chro
    15:15; Ezra 10:1; Nehe
    Psalm 85:6; Lamentati
    36:26; Hosea 6:6, 10:
    Habakkuk 3:2; Zecha

Salvation—Exodus 12:1
    Psalm 23:1, 27:1; I
    Jeremiah 17:7–8,
    Amos 5:4; Matth
    19:10; John 3:3,
    Acts 15:11, 16:3
    2 Corinthians 8
    Ephesians 1:7,
    Titus 3:5; Hel
    1 John 5:11–

Sin—Genesis 3
    23:1; Levit
    2 Samuel
    2 Kings 1
    Proverbs
    Jonah 1
    Titus 1

Succe
    M
    10:
    12:
    4:1
    2 Ti
    3 Jo

Tongue,
    15:1,
    2 Tim

Truth—E

Wisdom—
    1 Chro
    Esther 4
    Ecclesias
    1 Corint

Witnessing—
    Matthew
    1 Corinth
    Jude 3

Worship—Ger
    33:15; Levi

1 Chronicles 16:7, 23:30; 2 Chronicles 5:13;
Psalm 100:4–5, 103:1–2, 136:1–2;
Isaiah 29:13; Daniel 4:34; Malachi 1:6;
Luke 4:16, 5:8; Acts 14:15; Hebrews 10:25;
Revelation 4:11

Youth—Ecclesiastes 12:1

Inspirational Library

Beautiful purse/pocket-size editions of Christian classics bound in flexible leatherette. These books make thoughtful gifts for everyone on your list, including yourself!

When I'm on My Knees The highly popular collection of devotional thoughts on prayer, especially for women.
Flexible Leatherette. $4.97

The Bible Promise Book Over 1,000 promises from God's Word arranged by topic. What does God promise about matters like: Anger, Illness, Jealousy, Love, Money, Old Age, and Mercy? Find out in this book!
Flexible Leatherette. $3.97

Daily Wisdom for Women A daily devotional for women seeking biblical wisdom to apply to their lives. Scripture taken from the New American Standard Version of the Bible.
Flexible Leatherette. $4.97

My Daily Prayer Journal Each page is dated and features a Scripture verse and ample room for you to record your thoughts, prayers, and praises. One page for each day of the year.
Flexible Leatherette. $4.97

Available wherever books are sold.
Or order from:

Barbour Publishing, Inc.
P.O. Box 719
Uhrichsville, OH 44683
http://www.barbourbooks.com

If you order by mail, add $2.00 to your order for shipping.
Prices are subject to change without notice.